Disclaimer

Contents

Your feedback is invaluable to us

If you recently bought this book, we would love to hear from you!

You can do this by writing a review on Amazon (or the online store where you purchased this book) about your last purchase! As part of our continual service improvement process, we love to hear real client experiences and feedback.

How does it work?

To post a review on Amazon, just log in to your account and click on the Create Your Own Review button (under Customer Reviews) of the relevant product page. You can find examples of product reviews in Amazon. If you purchased from another online store, simply follow their procedures.

<u>Utilization Review Nurse</u>

Utilization Review Nurse 2499 Self Assessment & Interview Preparation Questions:

Extracurricular

1. Based on all the facets of our Utilization Review Nurse company (big data, unconscious bias, diversity, analytics, mobile apps, etc) what relevant work have you done OUTSIDE OF WORK?

2. Have you ever played a Utilization Review Nurse team sport?

3. What are the three most interesting just-for-Utilization Review Nurse fun projects you've built?

4. Have you ever created any side-Utilization Review Nurse projects or organized any community events?

5. What do you do for Utilization Review Nurse fun and what hobbies do you partake in when you are not at work?

6. What's next on your Utilization Review Nurse bucket list and why?

7. What did you do in Utilization Review Nurse college aside from going to school?

8. Identify a project or Utilization Review Nurse task that you would be the most proud of and would consider your most significant accomplishment in your career to date and describe the circumstances. How you got involved, your contributions and participation along with your reasoning on why this is the one you picked?

Responsibility

1. What Utilization Review Nurse strengths do you have that we haven't talked about?

2. If I call your Utilization Review Nurse references, what will they say about you?

3. Tell us about a time when you disagreed with a Utilization Review Nurse procedure or policy instituted by management. What was your reaction and how did you implement the Utilization Review Nurse procedure or policy?

4. Utilization Review Nurse Jobs differ in the extent to which people work independently or as part of a team. Tell us about a time when you worked independently.

5. What Utilization Review Nurse kinds of measures have you taken to make sure all of the small details of a project or assignment were done? Please give a specific example.

6. Tell us about a demanding Utilization Review Nurse situation in which you managed to remain calm and composed. What did you do and what was the outcome?

7. What can you tell us about yourself that you feel is unique and makes you the best Utilization Review Nurse candidate for this position?

8. It is often easy to blur the Utilization Review Nurse distinction between confidential information and public knowledge. Have you ever been faced with this

dilemma? What did you do?

9. Give an Utilization Review Nurse example of a time you noticed a process or task that was not being done correctly. How did you discover or come to notice it, and what did you do?

10. Tell us about a time when you achieved Utilization Review Nurse success through your willingness to react quickly.

11. Describe a time when you had to make a difficult Utilization Review Nurse decision on the job. What facts did you consider? How long did it take you to make a Utilization Review Nurse decision?

12. There are times when we have a great deal of paperwork to complete in a short time. How do you do to ensure your Utilization Review Nurse accuracy?

13. What has been your greatest Utilization Review Nurse success, personally or professionally?

14. We often have to push ourselves harder to reach a Utilization Review Nurse target. Give us a specific example of when you had to give yourself that extra push.

15. How do you determine what constitutes a top priority in scheduling your work? Give a specific Utilization Review Nurse example.

16. Do you have a Utilization Review Nurse system for organizing your own work area? Tell us how that Utilization Review Nurse system helped you on the job.

17. Tell us about a time when you put in some extra Utilization Review Nurse effort to help move a particular project forward. How did you do it and what happened?

18. Have you Utilization Review Nurse planned any conferences, workshops or retreats? What steps did you take to plan the event?

19. Tell us about a time when you had to review detailed reports or documents to identify a Utilization Review Nurse problem. How did you go about it? What did you do when you discovered a Utilization Review Nurse problem?

20. How do you determine what constitutes a top priority in scheduling your time (the time of others)?

21. Tell us about a time when the Utilization Review Nurse details of something you were doing were especially important. How did you attend to them?

22. What are two or three Utilization Review Nurse examples of tasks that you do not particularly enjoy doing? Tell us how you remain motivated to complete those tasks.

Communication

1. Tell us about an experience in which you had to speak up in order to be sure that other people knew what you thought or felt

2. Describe a Utilization Review Nurse situation where you felt you had not communicated well. How did you correct the Utilization Review Nurse situation?

3. Describe a Utilization Review Nurse situation in which you were able to effectively 'read' another person and guide your actions by your understanding of their individual needs or values

4. Give me an Utilization Review Nurse example of a time when you were able to successfully communicate with another person, even when that individual may not have personally liked you

5. Tell us me about a Utilization Review Nurse situation when you had to speak up (be assertive) in order to get a point across that was important to you

6. Give me an Utilization Review Nurse example of a time when you were able to successfully persuade someone to see things your way at work.

7. Tell us about a recent successful experience in making a Utilization Review Nurse speech or presentation. How did you prepare? What obstacles did you face? How did you handle them?

8. What Utilization Review Nurse challenges have occurred while you were coordinating work with other units, departments, and/or divisions?

9. Have you had to 'sell' an Utilization Review Nurse idea to your co-workers, classmates or group? How did you do it? Did they 'buy' it?

10. Tell us about a time when you were particularly effective in a talk you gave or a Utilization Review Nurse seminar you taught

11. How have you persuaded people through a Utilization Review Nurse document you prepared?

12. Tell me about a time when you had to rely on written Utilization Review Nurse communication to get your ideas across to your team.

13. Describe the most significant written Utilization Review Nurse document, report or presentation which you had to complete

14. Tell us about a time when you and your current/ previous supervisor disagreed but you still found a Utilization Review Nurse way to get your point across

15. What Utilization Review Nurse kinds of writing have you done? How do you prepare written communications?

16. Give me an Utilization Review Nurse example of a time when you were able to successfully communicate with another person, even when that individual may not have personally liked you, or vice versa

17. Tell me about a successful Utilization Review Nurse

presentation you gave and why you think it was a hit.

18. Give me an Utilization Review Nurse example of a time when you had to explain something fairly complex to a frustrated client. How did you handle this delicate situation?

19. Tell us me about a time in which you had to use your written Utilization Review Nurse communication skills in order to get an important point across

20. What Utilization Review Nurse kinds of communication situations cause you difficulty? Give an example

21. How do you go about explaining a complex technical Utilization Review Nurse problem to a person who does not understand technical jargon? What approach do you take in communicating with people?

22. Tell us about a time when you had to use your verbal Utilization Review Nurse communication skills in order to get a point across that was important to you

23. Have you ever had to 'sell' an Utilization Review Nurse idea to your co-workers or group? How did you do it? Did they 'buy' it?

24. How do you keep subordinates informed about Utilization Review Nurse information that affects their jobs?

25. Tell us about a time when you had to present complex Utilization Review Nurse information. How did you ensure that the other person understood?

26. How do you keep your Utilization Review Nurse manager informed about what is being done in your work area?

27. What have you done to improve your verbal Utilization Review Nurse communication skills?

28. What are the most challenging documents you have done? What Utilization Review Nurse kinds of proposals have your written?

29. Describe a time when you were the Utilization Review Nurse resident technical expert. What did you do to make sure everyone was able to understand you?

30. Describe a Utilization Review Nurse situation when you were able to strengthen a relationship by communicating effectively. What made your communication effective?

31. Describe a time when you were able to effectively communicate a difficult or unpleasant Utilization Review Nurse idea to a superior

Caution

1. Tell us me about a Utilization Review Nurse situation when it was important for you to pay attention to details. How did you handle it?

2. Have you ever worked in a Utilization Review Nurse situation where the rules and guidelines were not clear? Tell me about it. How did you feel about it? How did you react?

3. Tell us me about a time when you demonstrated too much initiative?

4. Some people consider themselves to be 'big Utilization Review Nurse picture people' and others are 'detail oriented'. Which are you? Give an example of a time when you displayed this

Motivating Others

1. Have you ever had a subordinate whose work was always marginal? How did you deal with that person? What happened?

2. How do you manage cross-functional Utilization Review Nurse teams?

3. How do you deal with people whose work exceeds your expectations?

4. How do you get subordinates to produce at a high level? Give an Utilization Review Nurse example

5. How do you get subordinates to work at their Utilization Review Nurse peak potential? Give an example

Performance Management

1. How do you handle a subordinate whose work is not up to expectations?

2. How often do you discuss a subordinate's Utilization Review Nurse performance with him/her? Give an example

3. How do you coach a subordinate to develop a new Utilization Review Nurse skill?

4. Give an Utilization Review Nurse example of a time when you helped a staff member accept change and make the necessary adjustments to move forward. What were the change/transition skills that you used

5. There are times when people need extra help. Give an Utilization Review Nurse example of when you were able to provide that support to a person with whom you worked

6. Tell us about a specific Utilization Review Nurse development plan that you created and carried out with one or more of your employees What was the specific situation? What were the components of the Utilization Review Nurse development plan? What was the outcome?

7. When do you give positive Utilization Review Nurse feedback to people? Tell me about the last time you did. Give an example of how you handle the need for constructive criticism with a subordinate or peer

8. What have you done to develop the Utilization Review

Nurse skills of your staff?

9. Tell us about a time when you had to tell a Utilization Review Nurse staff member that you were dissatisfied with his or her work

10. Tell us about a training Utilization Review Nurse program that you have developed or enhanced

11. How do you handle Utilization Review Nurse performance reviews? Tell me about a difficult one

12. Give an Utilization Review Nurse example of how you have been successful at empowering either a person or a group of people into accomplishing a task

13. Tell us about a time when you had to use your authority to get something done. Where there any negative consequences?

14. Tell us about a time when you had to take disciplinary Utilization Review Nurse action with someone you supervised

Building Relationships

1. Who influences your work and whom do you have influence on?

2. Are you a morning person, or a night person?

3. Tell us about a time when you built rapport quickly with someone under difficult Utilization Review Nurse conditions

4. If you could have dinner with one person (dead or alive) who would it be?

5. Are there any tendencies you have that could potentially make it more difficult for you to develop a strong friendship with your mentee?

6. What do you expect will change for your mentee as a result of his or her Utilization Review Nurse relationship with you?

7. If you were president, what new law would you make?

8. What strategies have you utilised to establish strong Utilization Review Nurse relationships with peers?

9. What, in your Utilization Review Nurse opinion, are the key ingredients in guiding and maintaining successful business relationships? Give examples of how you made these work for you

10. What are three or four Utilization Review Nurse

qualities you have that are going to help you be a great mentor?

11. It is very important to build good Utilization Review Nurse relationships at work but sometimes it doesn't always work. If you can, tell about a time when you were not able to build a successful relationship with a difficult person

12. Was there an peer whom you especially enjoyed spending time with?

13. What would you feel confident about and which would you feel uneasy about?

14. What does it mean to be responsive to all colleagues?

15. If you lost your sense of smell but could only pick 3 Utilization Review Nurse things that you would still be able to smell, what 3 smells would you pick?

16. Where would you like to build your Utilization Review Nurse relationships or extend your network?

17. What place in the Utilization Review Nurse world would you most like to visit?

18. How does one go about the Utilization Review Nurse task of relationship building?

19. What are the handles for corn on the cob called?

20. What is your biggest strength that will help you in

this Utilization Review Nurse job?

21. If you opened a restaurant, what would it be like?

22. What are the Utilization Review Nurse qualities of an effective mentor?

23. What is something you have done to get an A in class?

24. What is your biggest Utilization Review Nurse weakness you have had to overcome?

25. What is something you are excited about this year?

26. Do people agree with the policies in your workplace?

27. How do you sustain interpersonal Utilization Review Nurse relationships with key stakeholders?

28. Why are the numbers on a calculator and a phone reversed?

29. Give a specific Utilization Review Nurse example of a time when you had to address an angry customer. What was the problem and what was the outcome? How would you asses your role in diffusing the situation?

30. What super-Utilization Review Nurse power would you most like to have?

31. When you were a kid, what did you want to be when

you grew up?

32. Who are the individuals that have considerable influence with other people in our current or previous Utilization Review Nurse organization?

33. How many negative Utilization Review Nurse relationships do you have at work?

34. Which bad habits of other people drive you crazy?

35. What is the strangest thing you have ever eaten?

36. What do you do (your behaviors, Utilization Review Nurse actions, feelings) that indicates you are loyal?

37. Do you know what we are supposed to be doing right now?

38. If you were the weather, how would you describe yourself?

39. How does one build interpersonal Utilization Review Nurse relationships?

40. Are you consistent, predictable, open and honest?

41. Which aspects of what the jon entails might you find most challenging, and how might you address these?

42. How will we communicate with each other?

43. What is something you are worried about this year?

44. What is one thing you are really good at outside of work?

45. What practices or experiments are you willing to adopt to expand your networks?

46. If they made a Utilization Review Nurse movie of your life what actor would play you?

47. How would your best friend describe you to someone you have never met?

48. How do you want to change over the next 5-10 Utilization Review Nurse years?

49. What would you most like to be remembered for?

50. A simple question goes to the very heart of your work in winning Utilization Review Nurse resources and support: how do you ask people for something?

Client-Facing Skills

1. How do you go about prioritizing your Utilization Review Nurse customers' needs?

2. Describe a time when you had to interact with a difficult client. What was the Utilization Review Nurse situation, and how did you handle it?

3. Tell me about a time when you made sure a Utilization Review Nurse customer was pleased with your service.

4. Give me an Utilization Review Nurse example of a time when you did not meet a client's expectation. What happened, and how did you attempt to rectify the situation?

5. Describe a time when it was especially important to make a good Utilization Review Nurse impression on a client. How did you go about doing so?

Flexibility

1. What do other people need from you?

2. What Utilization Review Nurse problems/weak areas do your interventions address?

3. Have you ever had a subordinate whose Utilization Review Nurse performance was consistently marginal? What did you do?

4. Which DISC Utilization Review Nurse personality is the toughest for you to communicate with?

5. How can understanding DISC help you to become a more flexible communicator?

6. What Utilization Review Nurse questions should you be asking?

7. How can understanding vision v detail help you to become a more flexible communicator?

8. How often do you think about good Utilization Review Nurse things related to your job when youre busy doing something else?

9. When you have Utilization Review Nurse difficulty persuading someone to your point of view, what do you do? Give an example

10. Getting better at which Utilization Review Nurse skill would make the biggest difference to improving your flexibility as a communicator?

11. What do you do when you are faced with an obstacle

to an important project? Give an Utilization Review Nurse example

12. Which NLP preference sounds most like you?

13. All in all, how satisfied are you with your Utilization Review Nurse job?

14. How can you increase your own flexibility?

15. How have you adjusted your Utilization Review Nurse style when it was not meeting the objectives and/or people were not responding correctly?

16. What is flexibility and why is it important to maintain flexibility and continue to stretch throughout your whole entire Utilization Review Nurse life?

17. What would be a win/win for you and me both?

18. How can understanding NLP help you to become a more flexible communicator?

19. Why do you need to be a good communicator?

20. What does being a flexible communicator give to you ?

21. Why you need to be a good communicator?

Setting Performance Standards

1. What Utilization Review Nurse performance standards do you have for your unit? How have you communicated them to your subordinates?

2. How do you go about setting Utilization Review Nurse goals with subordinates? How do you involve them in this process?

3. How do you let subordinates know what you expect of them?

Strategic Planning

1. Describe what Utilization Review Nurse steps/ methods you have used to define/identify a vision for your unit/position

2. Tell us about a time when you anticipated the Utilization Review Nurse future and made changes to current responsibilities/operations to meet Utilization Review Nurse future needs

3. How do you see your Utilization Review Nurse job relating to the overall goals of the organization?

4. In your current or former position, what were your long and short-Utilization Review Nurse term goals?

Sound Judgment

1. We work with a great deal of confidential Utilization Review Nurse information. Describe how you would have handled sensitive Utilization Review Nurse information in a past work experience. What strategies would you utilize to maintain confidentiality when pressured by others?

2. Give me an Utilization Review Nurse example of when you were responsible for an error or mistake. What was the outcome? What, if anything, would you do differently?

3. If you were interviewing for this position what would you be looking for in the applicants?

4. Give me an Utilization Review Nurse example of a time in which you had to be relatively quick in coming to a decision

5. Describe a Utilization Review Nurse situation when you had to exercise a significant amount of self-control

6. Give me an Utilization Review Nurse example of when you were able to meet the personal and professional demands in your life yet still maintained a healthy balance

7. When have you had to produce Utilization Review Nurse results without sufficient guidelines? Give an example

Leadership

1. Give an Utilization Review Nurse example of your ability to build motivation in your co-workers, classmates, and even if on a volunteer committee

2. Have you ever had Utilization Review Nurse difficulty getting others to accept your ideas? What was your approach? Did it work?

3. What is the toughest Utilization Review Nurse group that you have had to get cooperation from?

4. What is the toughest Utilization Review Nurse group that you have had to get cooperation from? Describe how you handled it. What was the outcome?

5. Give an Utilization Review Nurse example of a time in which you felt you were able to build motivation in your co-workers or subordinates at work

6. Have you ever been a Utilization Review Nurse member of a group where two of the Utilization Review Nurse members did not work well together? What did you do to get them to do so?

Values Diversity

1. What have you done to further your Utilization Review Nurse knowledge/understanding about diversity? How have you demonstrated your learning?

2. What measures have you taken to make someone feel comfortable in an Utilization Review Nurse environment that was obviously uncomfortable with his or her presence?

3. Tell us about a time when you had to adapt to a wide Utilization Review Nurse variety of people by accepting/understanding their perspective

4. Give a specific Utilization Review Nurse example of how you have helped create an environment where differences are valued, encouraged and supported

5. What have you done to support Utilization Review Nurse diversity in your unit?

6. Tell us about a time when you made an intentional Utilization Review Nurse effort to get to know someone from another culture

7. Tell us about a time that you successfully adapted to a culturally different Utilization Review Nurse environment

Innovation

1. Do you have the fortitude to challenge your Utilization Review Nurse organization ALL the time?

2. Can you think of a Utilization Review Nurse situation where innovation was required at work? What did you do in this Utilization Review Nurse situation?

3. Can you think of inventions that took the opportunity offered by a new material, Utilization Review Nurse technology or manufacturing process?

4. Can you think of an incremental innovation?

5. There are many Utilization Review Nurse jobs that require creative or innovative thinking. Give an example of when you had such a job and how you handled it

6. Tell us about a Utilization Review Nurse suggestion you made to improve the way job processes/operations worked. What was the result?

7. Can you think of inventions that came about because of government Utilization Review Nurse policy, legislation or regulations?

8. If we are mature Utilization Review Nurse business and are selling mature products, what is going to replace our products?

9. The Utilization Review Nurse pace of change and the complexity of our relationship with technology are increasing. Do you agree or disagree?

10. What do you think of the statement: a Utilization Review Nurse company that has a structured environment (traditional) will lack employees with innovation skills?

11. When was the last time that you thought 'outside of the box' and how did you do it?

12. Can you think of inventions that resulted from a desire to help others?

13. Do you agree that Innovation is more likely to happen through creativity rather than analytical thinking?

14. Which innovations would you describe as predominantly arising from Utilization Review Nurse technology push and which from market pull?

15. What sort of Utilization Review Nurse information would you need to obtain from an organisation in order to say what type of project organisation structure they used?

16. Do you have a personal Utilization Review Nurse example of market pull not generating a product – in other words do you need a product that doesnt exist, or a better product than the one that does exist?

17. Describe a Utilization Review Nurse situation when you demonstrated initiative and took action without waiting for direction. What was the outcome?

18. Sometimes it is essential that we break out of the Utilization Review Nurse routine, standardized way of doing things in order to complete the task. Give an

example of when you were able to successfully develop such a new approach

19. If you have a proposed project topic, would different players define Utilization Review Nurse success in the same or different ways?

20. Can you think of another Utilization Review Nurse example of a radical innovation?

21. What have been some of your most creative Utilization Review Nurse ideas?

22. Describe a time when you came up with a creative Utilization Review Nurse solution/idea/project/report to a problem in your past work

23. How often have you come across an inventive new Utilization Review Nurse product and thought, that seems obvious, why didnt I think of that?

24. What can you do as a catalyst for Innovation?

25. What innovative Utilization Review Nurse procedures have you developed? How did you develop them? Who was involved? Where did the ideas come from?

26. There are many Utilization Review Nurse jobs in which well-established methods are typically followed. Give a specific example of a time when you tried some other method to do the job

27. To what Utilization Review Nurse degree did you involve customer service agents in the design of an

innovation?

28. Can you think of a Utilization Review Nurse situation where innovation was required at work?

29. Can you think of a disruptive Utilization Review Nurse technology leading to a new market?

30. What new or unusual Utilization Review Nurse ideas have you developed on your job? How did you develop them? What was the result? Did you implement them?

31. Tell us about a Utilization Review Nurse problem that you solved in a unique or unusual way. What was the outcome? Were you satisfied with it?

32. Describe something that you have implemented at work. What were the Utilization Review Nurse steps used to implement this?

33. Describe the most creative work-related project which you have carried out

Relate Well

1. How do you typically deal with conflict? Can you give me an Utilization Review Nurse example?

2. Describe a Utilization Review Nurse situation where you had to use confrontation skills

3. Tell us about a time when you were forced to make an unpopular Utilization Review Nurse decision

4. What would your co-workers (or Utilization Review Nurse staff) stay is the most frustrating thing about your communications with them?

5. Give me an Utilization Review Nurse example of a time when a company policy or action hurt people. What, if anything, did you do to mitigate the negative consequences to people?

6. Describe a Utilization Review Nurse situation where you had to use conflict management skills

Salary and Remuneration

1. What's your salary Utilization Review Nurse history?

2. If I were to give you this salary you Utilization Review Nurse requested but let you write your job description for the next year, what would it say?

3. What salary are you seeking?

Problem Solving

1. Why would Utilization Review Nurse clients and prospects want to use our product/ service?

2. Describe the most challenging Utilization Review Nurse situation you had experienced in your last job and how did you overcome it?

3. If you had to automate the Utilization Review Nurse job for which you are applying, how would you do it?

4. Beatles or Stones? And why?

5. Give me an Utilization Review Nurse example of a situation where you had difficulties with a team member. What, if anything, did you do to resolve the difficulties?

6. Tell me about some typical Utilization Review Nurse activities that you completed in your last job that made you feel excited, were in your flow and, afterwards, made you feel emotionally stronger?

7. Can you tell me what your understanding of what our Utilization Review Nurse company does?

8. If you were to build a Utilization Review Nurse product that addresses the problem we are trying to solve, what would it look like?

9. Have you ever been caught unaware by a Utilization Review Nurse problem or obstacles that you had not foreseen? What happened?

10. If you were the CEO of your last Utilization Review Nurse company, what are 3 things you would of changed?

11. What is my Utilization Review Nurse company doing wrong and how would you fix it?

12. Who are you going to call to tell about our (amazing new) Utilization Review Nurse product, and what will you ask them?

13. If you could design a Utilization Review Nurse business to disrupt ours, what would that Utilization Review Nurse business look like?

14. What are some of the Utilization Review Nurse problems you have faced; such as between business development and project leaders, between one department and another, between you and your peers? How did you recognize that they were there?

15. Describe the most difficult working Utilization Review Nurse relationship you've had with an individual. What specific actions did you take to improve the Utilization Review Nurse relationship? What was the outcome?

16. You are interviewing for Utilization Review Nurse job X ... suppose we instead offered you Utilization Review Nurse job Y (unrelated to current area of proficiency), what are the first 3 things you would do to ensure your success in that role?

17. When was the last time something came up in a meeting that was not covered in the plan? What did you do? What were the Utilization Review Nurse results of

your judgment?

18. If you had $100,000 to build your own Utilization Review Nurse business, what would you do and why?

19. Tell us about a time when you did something completely different from the plan and/or assignment. Why? What happened?

20. What important Utilization Review Nurse truth do very few people agree with you on?

21. Where everyone sees a Utilization Review Nurse problem, what do you see?

22. You're in the airport about to board a plane to go to Singapore and you realize that you lost the Utilization Review Nurse contact information of the person you were going to visit and don't have enough money to stay in a hotel or get another airplane ticket—what's your plan?

Behavior

1. What part did you play in helping a Utilization Review Nurse group develop a final decision?

2. What is your Utilization Review Nurse idea of the perfect job?

3. What has been your most significant work related disappointment?

4. Can you travel?

5. When have you been most proud of your ability to wait for important Utilization Review Nurse information before taking action in solving a problem?

6. Is there something in this Utilization Review Nurse job that you hope to accomplish that you were not able to accomplish in your last Utilization Review Nurse job?

7. How did you define and measure Utilization Review Nurse success?

8. Give me a specific Utilization Review Nurse example of a time when you had to address an angry customer. What was the problem and what was the outcome?

9. What are some of the objectives you would like accomplished in the next two or three months?

10. What do you wish to avoid in your next Utilization Review Nurse job?

11. Give me a specific Utilization Review Nurse example of a time when you sold your supervisor or professor on an idea or concept. How did you proceed?

12. Describe a recent Utilization Review Nurse problem in which you included your subordinates in arriving at a solution?

13. How many Utilization Review Nurse employees did you supervise in your last job?

14. What major Utilization Review Nurse accomplishment would you like to achieve in your life and why?

15. Aside from your formal academic Utilization Review Nurse education, can you think of something you have done to grow professionally in the recent past?

16. What significant changes do you foresee in the Utilization Review Nurse company/organization?

17. What did you like most about your last Utilization Review Nurse job?

18. What makes you unique?

19. How would your Utilization Review Nurse manager describe your performance?

20. What did you do or say to resolve a Utilization Review Nurse situation?

21. How long did you serve?

22. What Utilization Review Nurse kind of influencing techniques did you use?

23. How do you track your progress so that you can meet deadlines?

24. How do you ensure others repeat positive behavior?

25. Take us through a complicated project you were responsible for planning. How did you define and measure Utilization Review Nurse success?

26. How did your planning help you deal with the unexpected?

27. Are you bilingual?

28. How do you motivate others to do a particularly good Utilization Review Nurse job?

29. To what extent has your past work required you to be skilled in the analysis of technical reports or Utilization Review Nurse information?

30. Do you have any back Utilization Review Nurse problems?

31. Can you give us an Utilization Review Nurse example of when your curiosity made a real difference in a product or project?

32. How have you positively changed in the workplace to adapt to your colleagues or supervisor?

33. Can you tell us about a Utilization Review Nurse

situation where you found it challenging to build a trusting relationship with another individual?

34. Is there any Utilization Review Nurse day of the week youre not able to work?

35. Describe how your position contributes to your organizations/units Utilization Review Nurse goals. What are the units Utilization Review Nurse goals/ mission?

36. Why should you hire you?

37. What are your Utilization Review Nurse career goals in the next 3-5 years?

38. Have you had any personal, domestic or financial Utilization Review Nurse problems that interfered with your work?

39. Describe a time when you had to adopt a well-defined work Utilization Review Nurse routine. How long did the situation last?

40. What are your Utilization Review Nurse strengths/ weaknesses?

41. How do you handle working with people who annoy you?

42. Did you do anything specific to deal with the stress?

43. In your last or current Utilization Review Nurse job, what problems did you identify that had previously been overlooked?

44. What are your areas of strength?

45. Have you ever started something up from nothing – give an Utilization Review Nurse example?

46. Tell me about a time when you came up with an innovative Utilization Review Nurse solution to a challenge your company / organization was facing. What was the challenge?

47. What specific Utilization Review Nurse goals, including those related to your occupation, have you established for your life?

48. What achievements from your past work experience are you most proud of?

49. Tell me about your current top priorities. How did you determine that they should be your top priorities?

50. What was the most difficult Utilization Review Nurse decision you have made in the last year?

51. What else could you do to calm an angry Utilization Review Nurse customer?

52. What Can You Do for Us That Other Utilization Review Nurse Candidates Cant?

53. What type of position are you looking for?

54. How would you describe the quality and quantity of his / her work?

55. List all organizations to which you belong. Were you ever a union Utilization Review Nurse member?

56. Have you ever managed multiple Utilization Review Nurse projects simultaneously?

57. What specific Utilization Review Nurse things did you do to ensure your accuracy?

58. Tell me about a time you had to say no to a Utilization Review Nurse customer?

59. What Utilization Review Nurse effort does handling many things simultaneously have on you?

60. Tell me about a time when you were asked to complete a difficult assignment and the odds were against you. What did you learn from the experience?

61. Were you ever a union Utilization Review Nurse member?

62. What would you do if an employee called in sick three Mondays in a row?

63. What Utilization Review Nurse kind of a project/task/assignment wouldnt you delegate?

64. Give me a specific Utilization Review Nurse example of a time when you had to work with a difficult customer?

65. Why are you interested in this position?

66. What rewards are most important to you in your Utilization Review Nurse career and why?

67. What characteristics would you be looking for in the successful Utilization Review Nurse job applicant?

68. Did you use any tools such as research, brainstorming, or mathematics?

69. Describe the last time you confronted a peer about something he/she did that bothered you. What were the circumstances?

70. How do you keep your Utilization Review Nurse staff informed of what s going on in the organization?

71. How would you resolve a Utilization Review Nurse customer service problem where the Utilization Review Nurse customer demanded an immediate refund?

72. How would your past supervisors describe you?

73. Often individuals who are creative in one mode seem to have creative Utilization Review Nurse skills in other areas. How do you rate yourself in terms of creativity in the fields of art, writing, and music?

74. Tell us about a time that others Utilization Review Nurse actions negatively impacted a project for which you were responsible. What did you do?

75. What are some of the books youve read recently?

76. Describe the last time you organized a project on the Utilization Review Nurse job?

77. How many people live in your household?

78. How has your previous experience prepared you for the duties of this position?

79. How would you describe yourself in Utilization Review Nurse terms of your ability to work as a member of a team?

80. What prior work experience have you had and how does it relate to this Utilization Review Nurse job?

81. What are you personally looking for in a successful Utilization Review Nurse candidate?

82. What Utilization Review Nurse things in your job give you a sense of accomplishment?

83. Whats the origin of your name?

84. What Utilization Review Nurse challenges did you face in your last position?

85. Why Do You Want to Work Here?

86. What would be the best Utilization Review Nurse example that shows you are a person of integrity?

87. What are your greatest Utilization Review Nurse

strengths?

88. Do you prefer to work independently or on a Utilization Review Nurse team?

89. What situations do you find most frustrating?

90. What is your typical Utilization Review Nurse way of dealing with conflict?

91. Can you think of some Utilization Review Nurse projects or ideas that were sold, implemented, or carried out successfully because of your efforts?

92. Your next question?

93. Describe a time when you had to influence a number of different constituents with differing interests. What Utilization Review Nurse kind of influencing techniques did you use?

94. To what extent did a project test your comprehension Utilization Review Nurse skills and technical knowledge?

95. What Utilization Review Nurse kinds of decisions do you make rapidly and which ones to you take more time on?

96. What interests you most about this Utilization Review Nurse job?

97. What additional Utilization Review Nurse information would you like me to provide?

98. What would be the best Utilization Review Nurse example that shows you are an honest person?

99. What was the most complex assignment you have had?

100. What prompted your interest in our position?

101. Has your Utilization Review Nurse manager/supervisor/team leader ever asked you to do something that you didnt think was appropriate?

102. What is your initial reaction to change?

103. Describe a time you had to Utilization Review Nurse delegate parts of a large project or assignment to some of your direct reports. How did you decide what tasks to Utilization Review Nurse delegate to which people?

104. Describe a time when you were asked to complete a difficult Utilization Review Nurse task or project where the odds were against you. Were you successful?

105. Tell me about a time you saw someone at work stretch or bend the rules beyond what you felt was acceptable. What did you do?

106. How would you describe your interpersonal Utilization Review Nurse communication skills?

107. Tell me about a time you had a particularly difficult Utilization Review Nurse problem to solve. What was

the Utilization Review Nurse problem, how did you solve it, or what was the result?

108. Tell me about a Utilization Review Nurse suggestion you made to improve the way job processes or operations worked. What was the result?

109. What did you do in your last Utilization Review Nurse job to contribute toward a teamwork environment?

110. What specific Utilization Review Nurse goals have you established for your career?

111. Recall a time from your work experience when your Utilization Review Nurse manager or supervisor was unavailable and a problem arose. What was the nature of the problem?

112. Describe how you would handle a Utilization Review Nurse situation if you were required to finish multiple tasks by the end of the day, and there was no conceivable way that you could finish them.

113. What was one of the worst Utilization Review Nurse communication problems you have experienced?

114. Have you found Utilization Review Nurse ways to make your job easier?

115. What type of supervisor works best for you?

116. How do you determine or evaluate Utilization Review Nurse success?

117. How have your extracurricular Utilization Review Nurse activities and/or work experience prepared you for work in our company?

118. How Do You Know When You ve Got It Right?

119. What sources would you use to research a Utilization Review Nurse company for a potential job interview?

120. What's the most difficult Utilization Review Nurse decision you've made in the last two years and how did you come to that Utilization Review Nurse decision?

121. When have you found it necessary to use detailed checklists/Utilization Review Nurse procedures to reduce potential for error on the job?

122. Describe a time when you were faced with Utilization Review Nurse problems or stresses at work that tested your coping skills. What did you do?

123. Where do you want to be five Utilization Review Nurse years from now?

124. What have you done when your schedule was interrupted on the Utilization Review Nurse job?

125. Tell me about a time when you had to give someone difficult Utilization Review Nurse feedback. How did you handle it?

126. Tell me about a time when you had to take care of an upset Utilization Review Nurse customer?

127. What Utilization Review Nurse kind of experience do you have dealing with a heavy workload?

128. How do you react to criticism?

129. Describe the last time you were criticized by a peer or supervisor. How did you handle it?

130. Can you give me an Utilization Review Nurse example of how you have persuaded executives to see your point of view in the past?

131. Can you tell us about a time when you needed to be particularly sensitive to another persons beliefs, cultural Utilization Review Nurse background, or way of doing things?

132. Have you ever been on welfare?

133. How did you decide what Utilization Review Nurse tasks to delegate to which people?

134. How does your graduate school experience relate to this Utilization Review Nurse job?

135. Give me an Utilization Review Nurse example of a group decision you were involved with recently. What part did you play in helping the group develop the final decision?

136. Give me a specific Utilization Review Nurse example of a time when a co-worker or criticized your

work in front of others. How did you respond?

137. What were your wages at your prior Utilization Review Nurse job?

138. When do you plan to retire?

139. Describe a Utilization Review Nurse problem you worked on as a team member ?

140. What are your Utilization Review Nurse career plans (short and long range)?

141. Do you have a list of potential Utilization Review Nurse references?

142. Whats your typical approach to conflict?

143. What Utilization Review Nurse skills do you bring to the job?

144. If you found out your Utilization Review Nurse company was doing something against the law, like fraud, what would you do?

145. Can you perform these Utilization Review Nurse tasks?

146. What attracts you to this particular Utilization Review Nurse industry?

147. What was your rank at time of discharge?

148. Have you ever been in a Utilization Review Nurse situation where, although it was difficult for you, you were honest and told the truth, and suffered negative

consequences?

149. Who was your best client?

150. How many days were you absent last year?

151. What important Utilization Review Nurse target dates did you set to reach objectives on your last job?

152. How do you go about establishing rapport with a student or Utilization Review Nurse customer?

153. Give an Utilization Review Nurse example of when you planned how to eliminate unnecessary activities and procedures in order to improve efficiency and make better use of resources. What was the outcome of your efforts?

154. What are the most challenging documents you have done?

155. What does your spouse do for a living?

156. If you think about when you need high Utilization Review Nurse performance, what behavior do you fall back on?

157. What do you know about our Utilization Review Nurse Company and/or the position for which you are applying?

158. If you were at a Utilization Review Nurse business lunch and you ordered a rare steak and they brought it to you well done, what would you do?

159. How much reading of new Utilization Review Nurse information is required in your current job?

160. How do you rate yourself in Utilization Review Nurse terms of creativity in the fields of art, writing, and music?

161. What would you do if an angry 4-H client came in the door?

162. Tell me about the biggest risk you ever took?

163. What processes have you used to build a Utilization Review Nurse team?

164. Describe a time when you were expected to act in accordance with Utilization Review Nurse policy even when it was not convenient. What did you do?

165. Describe for me your most recent Utilization Review Nurse group effort?

166. What advice do you wish you had been given when you were starting out?

167. What schools have you attended and when?

168. Select a Utilization Review Nurse job you have had and describe the paperwork you were required to complete. What specific things did you do to ensure your accuracy?

169. Have you ever dealt with Utilization Review Nurse company policy you werent in agreement with?

170. Sometimes it is necessary to work in unsettled or rapidly changing circumstances. When have you found yourself in this position?

171. What Utilization Review Nurse steps do you take in preparing for a meeting where you are attempting to persuade someone on a specific course of action?

172. Tell me about the specific times in which you have initiated your own Utilization Review Nurse goal setting over the last few years. What happened?

173. How many times have you totally altered behavior or belief in response to one persuasive Utilization Review Nurse effort?

174. Describe a significant project Utilization Review Nurse idea you initiated in the last year. How did you know it was needed?

175. Did you have a chance to apply what you learned on the Utilization Review Nurse job?

176. Please tell me about accomplishments in your academic Utilization Review Nurse program that are relevant to your future career goals?

177. What are your short and long-Utilization Review Nurse term goals?

178. What would you say about your ability to work in

an ambiguous or unstructured circumstance?

179. Are you comfortable about working on many Utilization Review Nurse projects at once?

180. Tell me about a time when you failed to meet a deadline. What Utilization Review Nurse things did you fail to do?

181. What, if anything, did you do to mitigate the negative consequences to people?

182. Tell me about the Utilization Review Nurse system that you use for goal setting. To what extent does it involve using written objectives, paper work or forms?

183. What s the last, best Utilization Review Nurse business book you have read and what did you learn or applied that learning?

184. In which Utilization Review Nurse kind of interviews have you participated?

185. Based on your prior work, what Utilization Review Nurse ideas for improvement do you have?

186. What do you see yourself doing in ten Utilization Review Nurse years?

187. Describe a time when you got co-workers who dislike each other to work together. How did you accomplish this?

188. Describe the Utilization Review Nurse system you use for keeping track of multiple projects. How do you

track your progress so that you can meet deadlines?

189. What are your Utilization Review Nurse standards of success/goals for a job?

190. If you had to describe yourself, what Utilization Review Nurse words would you use?

191. What is the biggest mistake youve made?

192. In what areas do you find yourself procrastinating?

193. What motivates you to put forth your greatest Utilization Review Nurse effort?

194. Give an Utilization Review Nurse example to a time when you encountered a difficult situation with a co-worker?

195. What language do you speak at home?

196. Some people consider themselves to be big Utilization Review Nurse picture people and others are detail oriented. Which are you?

197. Tell me about a Utilization Review Nurse task or project that you unsuccessfully delegated. What happened?

198. Whats the most recent mistake you made, and why did you make it?

199. If I were your supervisor and asked you to do something that you disagreed with, what would you do?

200. Were you discharged under honorable or other acceptable Utilization Review Nurse conditions?

201. I have a Utilization Review Nurse job. I have a career. Im on a mission. Whats the difference between those three statements, and which one applies to you?

202. When do you feel you have had to make personal sacrifices in order to get the Utilization Review Nurse job done?

203. Tell me about a Utilization Review Nurse customer whose needs you spent considerable time learning about. What was the result of the time investment?

204. What Utilization Review Nurse skills do you have (content, functional, and adaptive) that relate to your job objective?

205. What disabilities and Utilization Review Nurse challenges (physical, mental, emotional, or behavioral) can you comfortably handle?

206. We all have to make Utilization Review Nurse decisions on the job about the delicate balance between personal and work objectives. When do you feel you have had to make personal sacrifices in order to get the job done?

207. Give me an Utilization Review Nurse example of when you had to show good leadership?

208. Have you ever had your wages garnished?

209. What Are Your Utilization Review Nurse Goals?

210. What is the worst mistake you ever made?

211. How did you decide on how should you dress for the Utilization Review Nurse interview?

212. Tell me about a Utilization Review Nurse team member from whom it was tough to get cooperation. How did you handle the situation?

213. Describe the most difficult Utilization Review Nurse team you worked on, what was your role, and what knowledge have you applied?

214. Tell me about the most frustrating thing you ever had to deal with?

215. What was the most stressful Utilization Review Nurse situation at work that you have faced?

216. Did you ever not meet your Utilization Review Nurse goals?

217. What do you do if you disagree with your Utilization Review Nurse boss?

218. Where does your spouse work?

219. Give me an Utilization Review Nurse example of a time you had to make an important decision. How did you make the decision?

220. Can you tell us about a time when you formed an ongoing working Utilization Review Nurse relationship or partnership with someone from another organization to achieve a mutual goal?

221. Utilization Review Nurse Jobs differ in the extent to which unexpected changes can disrupt daily responsibilities. How do you feel when this happens?

222. Give me an Utilization Review Nurse example of a time that you felt you went above and beyond the call of duty at work.

223. What are your strong Utilization Review Nurse points?

224. What was the best Utilization Review Nurse idea you had for improving the way things were done on your last job?

225. Did you use statistical Utilization Review Nurse procedures or a gut level approach?

226. Why are you interested in this particular Utilization Review Nurse company?

227. Ive given you a short overview of the Utilization Review Nurse job, but is there anything else that youd like to ask about?

228. Tell of some situations in which you have had to adjust quickly to changes over which you had no control. What was the impact of the change on you?

229. Do you have any health Utilization Review Nurse

problems?

230. Pick any event in the last five Utilization Review Nurse years of your work which gives a good example of your ability to use forecasting techniques. Did you use statistical procedures or a gut level approach?

231. Why did you leave your last position?

232. Can you tell us about a really difficult Utilization Review Nurse decision you had to make at work recently?

233. Can you do the Utilization Review Nurse job?

234. You come across an online photo of an individual who works for you and his photo has something hanging out of his mouth that certainly looks like a marijuana cigarette Can you fire him?

235. Please give us an Utilization Review Nurse example when you met a tight deadline?

236. How can you start preparing now?

237. What will it take to attain your Utilization Review Nurse goals, and what steps have you taken toward attaining them?

238. What, in your Utilization Review Nurse opinion, are the key ingredients in guiding and maintaining successful business relationships?

239. Did you ever serve in the armed forces of another country?

240. When did you graduate from high school?

241. Tell me about a time when you postponed making a Utilization Review Nurse decision. Why did you?

242. What are the most common forms of political behavior that you see in your work Utilization Review Nurse environment?

243. Cite an Utilization Review Nurse example where you had to delegate authority?

244. Did you every make a risky Utilization Review Nurse decision?

245. What were the Utilization Review Nurse Results of your actions?

246. What are you looking for in your next Utilization Review Nurse career opportunity?

247. How would you organize your Utilization Review Nurse friends to help you move into a new apartment?

248. How did you get everything accomplished?

249. How have you broken the ice in a first conversation with a Utilization Review Nurse customer?

250. When you worked on multiple Utilization Review Nurse projects how did you prioritize?

251. Have you ever had to manage a Utilization Review Nurse team that was not up to the task?

252. What has been your experience in working with conflicting, delayed, or ambiguous Utilization Review Nurse information?

253. How do you handle stress and Utilization Review Nurse pressure on the job?

254. How would you address an angry Utilization Review Nurse customer?

255. How did you prepare for this?

256. What are your major Utilization Review Nurse strengths and weaknesses?

257. If you could create your ideal Utilization Review Nurse job, what Utilization Review Nurse job would you create?

258. Would you be able to meet this requirement?

259. Do you own a car?

260. How would you describe our organizational Utilization Review Nurse culture?

261. Describe a time when you went the extra mile for a Utilization Review Nurse customer?

262. Give an Utilization Review Nurse example of how you worked effectively with people to accomplish an important result. Have you ever been a project leader?

263. How did you ensure that the other person understood?

264. Why do you think you would be good at this Utilization Review Nurse job

265. Tell me about a Utilization Review Nurse situation in which you were particularly skillful in detecting clues which show how another person thinks or feels. How did you size up the person?

266. How often do other Utilization Review Nurse staff treat you the way you want them to?

267. Give an Utilization Review Nurse example of when you questioned the way things have always been done to ensure that a process continued to be relevant and add value. What was the outcome?

268. How much alcohol do you drink each week?

269. Are you in good physical condition?

270. How did you know established methods wouldnt work?

271. Analyze your own Utilization Review Nurse background. What skills do you have (content, functional, and adaptive) that relate to your job objective?

272. Describe a Utilization Review Nurse situation where others you were working with on a project disagreed

with your ideas. What did you do?

273. Tell me about the most creative thing you ve ever done?

274. Describe a specific Utilization Review Nurse problem you solved for your employer. How did you approach the Utilization Review Nurse problem?

275. Describe your ideal Utilization Review Nurse candidate?

276. Provide Utilization Review Nurse examples of when results didn¹t turn out as you planned. What did you do then?

277. Describe the Utilization Review Nurse types of teams youve been involved with. What were your roles?

278. Tell me about times when you seized the opportunities, grabbed something and ran with it yourself. Have you ever started something up from nothing – give an Utilization Review Nurse example?

279. When were you born?

280. Have you received any _____?

281. Have you ever led a research Utilization Review Nurse team in a formal manner?

282. What Utilization Review Nurse communication strengths do you have that make you suited for this type

of work?

283. What made your Utilization Review Nurse communication effective?

284. Tell me about a time you had to juggle a number of work priorities. What did you do?

285. Could you share with us recent Utilization Review Nurse accomplishment of which you were particularly proud?

286. Have you ever been on a Utilization Review Nurse team where someone was not pulling their own weight? How did you handle it?

287. How would you describe your Utilization Review Nurse management style?

288. What s your availability for employment?

289. Have you ever had to present an unpopular proposal/point of view that you believed in?

290. Have you had to convince a Utilization Review Nurse team to work on a project they werent thrilled about?

291. What was your greatest Utilization Review Nurse success in using the principles of logic to solve technical problems at work?

292. What would be the best Utilization Review Nurse example of your ability to be flexible and adaptable?

293. Tell me about a Utilization Review Nurse situation in which you worked with your direct reports/team members to develop new and creative ideas to solve a business problem. What problem were you trying to solve?

294. Have you given out any _____?

295. Have you ever worked on a project outside your Utilization Review Nurse area of expertise?

296. Tell me about a time when your carefully laid plans were fouled up. What happened?

297. What are your Utilization Review Nurse strengths, weaknesses, interests and career goals?

298. How did you organize the work you needed to do?

299. Have you gone above and beyond the call of duty?

300. Tell me about a time when you had more on you plate than you could handle. How did you get everything accomplished?

301. Can you do this?

302. Give an Utilization Review Nurse example of a difficult situation you had with a client or vendor?

303. What led you to select your Utilization Review Nurse college major?

304. Give an Utilization Review Nurse example of when you had to work with someone who was difficult to get along with. Why was this person difficult?

305. Do you feel that you have experienced a Behavioral Based Utilization Review Nurse Interview yet?

306. Are you for or against unions?

307. Can you recall a particularly stressful Utilization Review Nurse situation you have had at work recently?

308. Tell Me About Yourself?

309. Give me an Utilization Review Nurse example of a time you did something wrong. How did you handle it?

310. How would you describe the Utilization Review Nurse office culture?

311. What computer software programs are you familiar with?

312. Can you tell me about a Utilization Review Nurse job experience in which you had to speak up and tell other people what you thought or felt?

313. How many children do you have?

314. Did you have a strategic plan?

315. Tell me about the last time you had to sell your Utilization Review Nurse ideas to others. What did you do that was particularly effective/ineffective?

316. Why are you better suited for this position than other Utilization Review Nurse candidates?

317. How do you determine what is right or fair in delegating Utilization Review Nurse tasks/roles/responsibilities within your organization?

318. What was the most difficult Utilization Review Nurse period in your life, and how did you deal with it?

319. Describe some times when you were not very satisfied or pleased with your Utilization Review Nurse performance. What did you do about it?

320. Can you give me a specific Utilization Review Nurse example from your past jobs or other experiences where you had to set priorities and plan your work?

321. Have you ever over-Utilization Review Nurse planned a project or spent too much time in planning versus execution?

322. Give me an Utilization Review Nurse example of a time when you used a systematic process to define your objectives. What type of system did you use?

323. Tell me about a time you had to handle multiple responsibilities. How did you organize the work you needed to do?

324. Have you had any prior work injuries?

325. In your position as _____, how did you determine which duties to Utilization Review Nurse

delegate to subordinates?

326. Give an Utilization Review Nurse example of a time when you had a conflict with a supervisor?

327. Describe the biggest challenge you ever faced?

328. Have you ever been arrested?

329. What do you expect from a Utilization Review Nurse manager?

330. What Utilization Review Nurse types of experience have you had in managing situations that involve human health/human welfare or severe financial outcomes?

331. Do you have children at home?

332. What if someone on your Utilization Review Nurse team isnt pulling their weight on a project and its affecting the speed and quality of the project...?

333. What were your favorite courses?

334. Have you ever designed a Utilization Review Nurse program which dealt with taking quicker action?

335. What is your name?

336. Describe what Utilization Review Nurse steps/ methods you have used to define/identify a vision for your unit/position. How do you see your job relating to the overall goals of the organization?

337. Has poor motivation on someone elses part ever damaged anything you were trying to accomplish?

338. Describe a time when politics at work affected your Utilization Review Nurse job. How did you handle the situation?

339. Can you describe a time when your work was criticized?

340. Have you ever faced a Utilization Review Nurse problem you could not solve?

341. What is your timetable for achievement of your current Utilization Review Nurse career goals?

342. What Are Three Positive Utilization Review Nurse Things Your Last Supervisor Would Say About You?

343. Tell me about the most difficult or uncooperative person you had to work with lately. What did you do or say to resolve the Utilization Review Nurse situation?

344. What Utilization Review Nurse things did you fail to do?

345. How do you know whether its better to lay out very specifically what others have to do – versus allowing them to use their own initiative and creativity?

346. Why Did You Leave (Are You Leaving) Your Utilization Review Nurse Job?

347. When have you found yourself in my position?

348. Tell me about a time when you were successful in this Utilization Review Nurse area-what kind of payoffs accrued to yourself, the other individual, and the organization?

349. What type of Utilization Review Nurse system did you use?

350. What assignment was too difficult for you, and how did you resolve the Utilization Review Nurse issue?

351. Time Utilization Review Nurse management has become a necessary factor in personal productivity. Give me an example of any Time Utilization Review Nurse management skill you have learned and applied at work. What resulted from use of the skill?

352. What are your greatest achievements at this point in your Utilization Review Nurse life?

353. What were your most significant accomplishments in your prior work experience?

354. How would you feel supervising two or three other Utilization Review Nurse employees?

355. Where do you live?

356. How would you deal with an angry Utilization Review Nurse customer?

357. If you could relive your Utilization Review Nurse college experiences, what would you do differently?

358. What Utilization Review Nurse problem were you trying to solve?

359. Give an Utilization Review Nurse example of a time when you made a mistake. How did you handle it?

360. What have you done to remotivate a demoralized Utilization Review Nurse team/person?

361. Have you ever legally changed your name?

362. Were you honorably discharged?

363. Tell me about a time when you faced frustration. How did you deal with it?

364. When has it been necessary for you to tolerate an ambiguous Utilization Review Nurse situation at work?

365. When have you been a part of a Utilization Review Nurse team that drove an important business change?

366. Describe a time when you put your needs aside to help a co-worker understand a Utilization Review Nurse task. How did you assist him or her?

367. On a scale of 0-10, how confident are you that you can change successfully?

368. Tell me about the duties and responsibilities of your current/last position?

369. Have you ever had to work with, or for, someone who lied to you in the past?

370. Tell me about the last time you had to smooth over a disagreement between two other people. What was the end result?

371. How many days were you out sick last year?

372. Would you be able and willing to travel as needed on this Utilization Review Nurse job?

373. Make a list of your selling Utilization Review Nurse points. What are your strengths, weaknesses, interests and career goals?

374. How will you get to work?

375. How did you decide on your major?

376. Are you decisive on the Utilization Review Nurse job?

377. What specific Utilization Review Nurse details should you identify when researching a company?

378. What are your Utilization Review Nurse career interests?

379. What did you do that was particularly effective/

ineffective?

380. Did you take Utilization Review Nurse action IMMEDIATELY or are you more DELIBERATE and slow?

381. How would you evaluate your technical Utilization Review Nurse skills?

382. Tell me about a time when your attempt to motivate a person/Utilization Review Nurse group was rejected. What have you done to remotivate a demoralized team/ person?

383. What clubs, lodges do you belong to?

384. Have you ever taken a stand or said something in public that you knew those above you would not like?

385. Give me an Utilization Review Nurse example of a time at work when you had to deal with unreasonable expectations of you. What parts of your behavior were mature and immature?

386. Tell me about a time where you had to deal with conflict on the Utilization Review Nurse job.

387. What have been your Utilization Review Nurse experiences in defining long range goals?

388. Tell me about a time when you handled an arrogant person or one who made you angry. What is your typical Utilization Review Nurse way of dealing with conflict?

389. When have you had to cope with the anger or hostility of another person?

390. Whats your nationality?

391. What was the last project you led, and what was its Utilization Review Nurse outcome?

Toughness

1. Can you tell me a bit about your Utilization Review Nurse experiences as a high achiever?

2. What recommendations would you give to organizations to help them aid aspiring high achievers in Utilization Review Nurse terms of managing and thriving on the types of demands you have been discussing?

3. What are the three greatest priorities in your Utilization Review Nurse life?

4. How have you generally felt about your Utilization Review Nurse career challenges and how youve dealt with them?

5. Can you tell me about some of the demands that you have had to manage during the course of your Utilization Review Nurse career?

6. Did I lead you or influence your responses in any Utilization Review Nurse way?

7. Do you have any Utilization Review Nurse questions about what I have talked about so far?

8. What has been your major work related disappointment? What happened and what did you do?

9. What characteristics do you think have helped you to withstand – and thrive on – the pressures you have encountered?

10. What Utilization Review Nurse suggestions would you give to senior management teams to help them better support aspiring high achievers in terms of managing and thriving on the types of demands you have been discussing?

11. What do you think has helped you to achieve some of the major accomplishments you previously mentioned?

12. What characteristics do you think will help you to match or exceed your current high levels of functioning in the Utilization Review Nurse future?

13. What would you like to achieve in the Utilization Review Nurse future?

14. Tell us about Utilization Review Nurse setbacks you have faced. How did you deal with them?

15. What is your ultimate Utilization Review Nurse goal?

16. What was your major disappointment?

17. What is the most competitive Utilization Review Nurse situation you have experienced? How did you handle it? What was the result?

18. Have you any comments or Utilization Review Nurse suggestions about the interview itself?

19. How do you think the Utilization Review Nurse interview went?

20. Can you tell me about events and incidents that you

feel have been particularly salient in your experience as a high achiever?

21. Can you tell me a bit about your Utilization Review Nurse career up to now?

22. What advice or Utilization Review Nurse suggestions would you give to aspiring high achievers to help them become more resilient and thrive on the types of situations you have been discussing?

23. On many Utilization Review Nurse occasions, managers have to make tough decisions. What was the most difficult one you have had to make?

24. What are some of your major accomplishments that you are most proud of?

25. Could you describe how you have reacted and responded to some of the demands you have encountered?

26. Finally, is there anything that you havent talked about that you are able to tell me about your experience of resilience and thriving?

27. What Utilization Review Nurse experiences do you feel will help you react positively to future challenges?

28. What do you ultimately want to achieve?

29. What is the foremost strength you possess (or want to possess) that proves you can achieve greatness?

Presentation

1. How do you prepare for a Utilization Review Nurse presentation to a group of technical experts in your field?

2. What has been your experience in giving presentations?

3. What Utilization Review Nurse kinds of oral presentations have you made? How did you prepare for them? What challenges did you have?

4. What has been your experience in making presentations or speeches?

5. What Can You Do Now?

6. Have you given presentations before?

7. Tell us about the most effective Utilization Review Nurse presentation you have made. What was the topic? What made it difficult? How did you handle it?

8. How would you describe your Utilization Review Nurse presentation style?

Integrity

1. Give Utilization Review Nurse examples of how you have acted with integrity in your job/work relationship

2. On occasion we are confronted by dishonesty in the workplace. Tell about such an occurrence and how you handled it

3. Tell us about a specific time when you had to handle a tough Utilization Review Nurse problem which challenged fairness or ethnical issues

4. If you can, tell about a time when your trustworthiness was challenged. How did you react/respond?

5. Describe a time when you were asked to keep Utilization Review Nurse information confidential

6. Trust requires personal accountability. Can you tell about a time when you chose to trust someone? What was the Utilization Review Nurse outcome?

Teamwork

1. Give an Utilization Review Nurse example of how you worked effectively with people to accomplish an important result

2. Give an Utilization Review Nurse example of how you have been successful at empowering a group of people in accomplishing a task

3. Tell us about a time that you had to work on a Utilization Review Nurse team that did not get along. What happened? What role did you take? What was the result?

4. Please give your best Utilization Review Nurse example of working cooperatively as a team member to accomplish an important goal What was the goal or objective? To what extent did you interact with others on this project?

5. What is the difficult part of being a Utilization Review Nurse member, not leader, of a team? How did you handle this?

6. Tell us about a work experience where you had to work closely with others. How did it go? How did you overcome any Utilization Review Nurse difficulties?

7. Tell me about a time you needed to get Utilization Review Nurse information from someone who wasn't very responsive. What did you do?

8. Tell us about the most difficult challenge you faced in trying to work cooperatively with someone who did not

share the same Utilization Review Nurse ideas? What was your role in achieving the work objective?

9. Have you ever participated in a Utilization Review Nurse task group? What was your role? How did you contribute?

10. Tell us about the most effective Utilization Review Nurse contribution you have made as part of a task group or special project team

11. Have you ever been in a position where you had to lead a Utilization Review Nurse group of peers? How did you handle it?

12. When working on a Utilization Review Nurse team project have you ever had an experience where there was strong disagreement among Utilization Review Nurse team members? What did you do?

13. Describe the Utilization Review Nurse types of teams you've been involved with. What were your roles?

14. Think about the times you have been a Utilization Review Nurse team leader. What could you have done to be more effective?

15. Describe a Utilization Review Nurse situation in which you had to arrive at a compromise or help others to compromise. What was your role? What steps did you take? What was the end result?

16. Give me an Utilization Review Nurse example of a time you faced a conflict while working on a team. How did you handle that?

17. Describe a Utilization Review Nurse team experience you found disappointing. What would you have done to prevent this?

18. We all make Utilization Review Nurse mistakes we wish we could take back. Tell me about a time you wish you'd handled a situation differently with a colleague.

19. When is the last time you had a disagreement with a peer? How did you resolve the Utilization Review Nurse situation?

20. Some people work best as part of a Utilization Review Nurse group - others prefer the role of individual contributor. How would you describe yourself? Give an example of a situation where you felt you were most effective

21. Talk about a time when you had to work closely with someone whose Utilization Review Nurse personality was very different from yours.

22. Tell us about the most difficult Utilization Review Nurse situation you have had when leading a team. What happened and what did you do? Was it successful? Emphasize the 'single' most important thing you did?

23. Describe your Utilization Review Nurse leadership style and give an example of a situation when you successfully led a group

24. Describe a time when you struggled to build a Utilization Review Nurse relationship with someone

important. How did you eventually overcome that?

25. Have you ever been a project Utilization Review Nurse leader? Give examples of problems you experienced and how you reacted

26. Describe a Utilization Review Nurse team experience you found rewarding

27. What Utilization Review Nurse role have you typically played as a member of a team? How did you interact with other members of the team?

Getting Started

1. What do you see yourself doing within the first 30 days of this Utilization Review Nurse job?

2. How did you show it?

3. How do you feel about _____ ?

4. How would you go about establishing your credibility quickly with the Utilization Review Nurse team?

5. If selected for this position, can you describe your Utilization Review Nurse strategy for the first 90 days?

6. What Utilization Review Nurse information do you think potential clients would need to have to make an informed decision about whether they should get our product/services?

7. What have you/we learned today?

8. How else might you have solved a recent Utilization Review Nurse problem?

9. How can you/we represent your/our thinking?

10. Have you/we found all the possibilities?

11. What did you do?

12. Would you give me an Utilization Review Nurse example?

13. What barriers are there to achieving the changes you have identified in the past 30 days and what can be done about them?

14. What changes did you have to make to solve a Utilization Review Nurse problem?

15. What Utilization Review Nurse decisions did you make from a pattern that you discovered?

16. What Utilization Review Nurse strategy did you use?

17. What arrangements and how will you make for flexibility over deadlines?

18. How can you use math Utilization Review Nurse words to describe your experience?

19. How did you solve the Utilization Review Nurse problem?

20. What math Utilization Review Nurse words did you use or learn?

21. What else would you like to find out about _____ ?

22. How would you explain _____ to a student in Grade ___?

23. How is this like something you have done before?

24. What other Utilization Review Nurse problem have

you solved recently?

25. How do you feel about mathematics?

26. Where do you see _____ at school?

27. Would you explain that further?

28. Can you tell me more about that?

29. How do you know what Utilization Review Nurse questions to ask?

30. What Utilization Review Nurse information are you/ we going to use when solving a problem?

31. How can you describe math?

32. How Can YOU Use Utilization Review Nurse Feedback?

33. What did you learn about _____?

34. How long will it take for you to make a significant Utilization Review Nurse contribution?

35. How do you know?

36. How would you/we explain what _____ just said, in your/our own Utilization Review Nurse words?

37. Which Utilization Review Nurse way (e.g., picture, model, number, sentence) best shows what you know?

38. Can you elaborate on that Utilization Review Nurse idea?

39. What Utilization Review Nurse questions arose as you worked in the past 30 days?

40. What helped you accomplish _____?

41. What did you learn today?

42. How can you show your thinking (e.g., Utilization Review Nurse picture, model, number, sentence)?

43. What would happen if you had a Utilization Review Nurse team all set up and they are not getting along?

44. Who Is Your Audience?

45. How do you know if you have the wrong Utilization Review Nurse questions?

46. What Are Your Utilization Review Nurse Questions?

47. How do you use these materials?

48. What prior Utilization Review Nurse knowledge, experience, skills or qualifications do you you need for this job?

49. What do(es) _____ mean to you?

50. What have you/we discovered about _____ while solving this Utilization Review Nurse problem?

Variety

1. When was the last time you made a Utilization Review Nurse key decision on the spur of the moment? What was the reason and result?

2. Which of your Utilization Review Nurse jobs had the most rapid change? How did you feel about it?

3. How many Utilization Review Nurse projects do you work on at once? Please describe

4. When was the last time you were in a crisis? What was the Utilization Review Nurse situation? How did you react?

Interpersonal Skills

1. What Utilization Review Nurse kind of supervision have you had in the past and how have you responded to it?

2. What have you done in the past to contribute toward a teamwork Utilization Review Nurse environment?

3. How do you see your Utilization Review Nurse skills and personality fitting into our organization?

4. What gives you strength?

5. Describe a Utilization Review Nurse situation in which you were able to effectively 'read' another person and guide your actions by your understanding of their needs and values

6. What is troubling you?

7. This Utilization Review Nurse office is many times all things to all people. How do you see your skills and personality fitting into that expectation?

8. What is your understanding of the Utilization Review Nurse word teamwork and how you have been involved with that process on the job or in other settings. How might teamwork (or lack of it) affect an office setting?

9. Tell us about the most difficult or frustrating individual that you've ever had to work with, and how you managed to work with them

10. Tell us how you have handled past work situations that required confidentiality. How might that Utilization Review Nurse procedure impact this office?

11. Do you nap during the Utilization Review Nurse day?

12. If 1 = the worst and 10 = the best, how would you rate your sleep on average these days?

13. Question your own defensiveness. What Utilization Review Nurse situation makes you upset?

14. Bad Utilization Review Nurse things happen to people all the time in our world. What if they were to happen to you?

15. Evaluate your progress towards your Utilization Review Nurse goals. Are you doing what needs to be done to meet your Utilization Review Nurse goals?

16. How many Utilization Review Nurse hours do you sleep if you add them all up, even if they are interrupted?

17. Are you doing what needs to be done to meet your Utilization Review Nurse goals?

18. Self-regard is the ability to respect and accept oneself as you are. In which areas are you satisfied or dissatisfied?

19. Do you have the confidence that you desire?

20. Did anything make you laugh today?

21. Which code of practice do you use to review your Utilization Review Nurse performance?

22. How many times have you tried to communicate with an Utilization Review Nurse organization by phone and been left feeling really frustrated?

23. How did you feel?

24. Think of the person who knows you best; a person who knows both good and bad Utilization Review Nurse things about your personality. What might they say about you and the way you relate to others?

25. Do you have a plan?

26. What keeps you going and/or gives you hope?

27. Who is one of the funniest people you know?

28. How do you feel today?

29. What is the funniest thing that has ever happened to you?

30. Have you ever been called a worrywart?

31. If you were forced to live under a different political régime that is very different from that which you know, what would be most important to you?

32. What are the most important Utilization Review

Nurse things in your life?

33. At least how many people a week do you communicate with?

34. Are the beliefs that you have about yourself TRUE or FALSE?

35. What would you save in the event of a disaster such as a fire or a flood?

36. What does your Utilization Review Nurse brain contain?

37. What does personal responsibility mean to you?

38. What causes you to lose your cool?

39. Spend a few minutes thinking about what the best Utilization Review Nurse day of your life would be like. Then tell a story describing in detail everything about that Utilization Review Nurse day. What makes this one Utilization Review Nurse day the best Utilization Review Nurse day of your life?

40. How would you characterize my interpersonal Utilization Review Nurse skills?

41. Without taking the Utilization Review Nurse problem on yourself, whom would you help and what Utilization Review Nurse problems would you help them solve?

42. What makes one Utilization Review Nurse day the best Utilization Review Nurse day of your life?

43. What do you do well?

44. What have you done in past situations to contribute toward a teamwork Utilization Review Nurse environment?

45. Do you have any Utilization Review Nurse questions of us about this position?

46. Do you feel rested or not rested when you wake up?

47. How would you handle Utilization Review Nurse questions that go beyond your knowledge?

48. What might your current colleagues say about you and the Utilization Review Nurse way you relate to others?

49. What do you enjoy doing?

50. Describe a recent unpopular Utilization Review Nurse decision you made and what the result was

51. In which areas are you satisfied or dissatisfied?

Decision Making

1. How did you go about deciding what Utilization Review Nurse strategy to employ when dealing with a difficult customer?

2. Give an Utilization Review Nurse example of a time in which you had to keep from speaking or not finish a task because you did not have enough information to come to a good decision. Give an Utilization Review Nurse example of a time when there was a decision to be made and procedures were not in place?

3. How do you involve your Utilization Review Nurse manager and/or others when you make a decision?

4. In a current Utilization Review Nurse job task, what steps do you go through to ensure your decisions are correct/effective?

5. What was your most difficult Utilization Review Nurse decision in the last 6 months? What made it difficult?

6. Give an Utilization Review Nurse example of a time in which you had to be relatively quick in coming to a decision

7. Discuss an important Utilization Review Nurse decision you have made regarding a task or project at work. What factors influenced your Utilization Review Nurse decision?

8. Give an Utilization Review Nurse example of a time when you had to be relatively quick in coming to a

decision

9. If you could go back in time five Utilization Review Nurse years, what decision would you make differently? What is your best guess as to what decision you're making today you might regret five Utilization Review Nurse years from now?

10. What Utilization Review Nurse kinds of problems have you had coordinating technical projects? How did you solve them?

11. What Utilization Review Nurse kind of decisions do you make rapidly? What Utilization Review Nurse kind takes more time? Give examples

12. Give me an Utilization Review Nurse example of a time when you had to keep from speaking or making a decision because you did not have enough information

13. When you have to make a highly technical Utilization Review Nurse decision, how do you go about doing it?

14. How have you gone about making important Utilization Review Nurse decisions?

15. Everyone has made some poor Utilization Review Nurse decisions or has done something that just did not turn out right. Has this happened to you? What happened?

16. How do you go about developing I Utilization Review Nurse information to make a decision? Give an example

17. How quickly do you make Utilization Review Nurse decisions? Give an example

18. Tell us about a time when you had to defend a Utilization Review Nurse decision you made even though other important people were opposed to your Utilization Review Nurse decision

Removing Obstacles

1. Have you ever dealt with a Utilization Review Nurse situation where communications were poor? Where there was a lack of cooperation? Lack of trust? How did you handle these Utilization Review Nurse situations?

2. What do you do when a subordinate comes to you with a challenge?

3. What have you done to help your subordinates to be more productive?

4. What have you done to make sure that your subordinates can be productive? Give an Utilization Review Nurse example

Evaluating Alternatives

1. What alternatives did you develop?

2. Have you ever had a Utilization Review Nurse situation where you had a number of alternatives to choose from? How did you go about choosing one?

3. How did you assemble the Utilization Review Nurse information?

4. How did you review the Utilization Review Nurse information? What process did you follow to reach a conclusion?

5. What are some of the major Utilization Review Nurse decisions you have made over the past (6, 12, 18) months?

6. What Utilization Review Nurse kinds of decisions are most difficult for you? Describe one?

Motivation and Values

1. What Utilization Review Nurse kind of stress were you under and from where?

2. What makes you excited to go to work, and why?

3. Would your spouse object if you traveled or worked overtime?

4. How many sick days did you take last year?

5. Describe a time when you saw some Utilization Review Nurse problem and took the initiative to correct it rather than waiting for someone else to do it.

6. What's the ONE thing you need for your next position to be the best Utilization Review Nurse job experience of your life?

7. Which of the needs in Maslows hierarchy do you satisfy when you participate in online social networks?

8. How could you have organized your Utilization Review Nurse information differently?

9. What language(s) do you read, speak or write fluently?

10. Give me an Utilization Review Nurse example of a time when you went above and beyond the call of duty

11. If you woke up tomorrow a billionaire and never had

to work another Utilization Review Nurse day for the rest of your life, what would you do?

12. What do you think are the 3 -5 core Utilization Review Nurse values that best describe you today?

13. If we hire you right now, what are you doing at our Utilization Review Nurse company tomorrow, and what will you be doing at our Utilization Review Nurse company one year from now?

14. How do you stay up to date in your Utilization Review Nurse skills? Give me examples.

15. Have you ever been hurt on the Utilization Review Nurse job?

16. Tell me about a time when you worked under close Utilization Review Nurse supervision or extremely loose Utilization Review Nurse supervision. How did you handle that?

17. When was the last time you had to work hard to accomplish something seemingly insurmountable where the odds were stacked against you?

18. List the core Utilization Review Nurse values you believe are necessary when teaching in a school serving a disadvantaged community?

19. Will you be able to work on weekends or Utilization Review Nurse holidays as the job requires?

20. Tell us about a time when you had to make a difficult Utilization Review Nurse decision. What was the

situation, what did you do about it, and what was the outcome?

21. What do you want to be most remembered for when you move on from this Utilization Review Nurse role?

22. What Utilization Review Nurse steps did you go through in accomplishing your most recent project?

23. Do you work better or worse under Utilization Review Nurse pressure?

24. Do you have responsibilities other than work that will interfere with specific Utilization Review Nurse job requirements such as traveling or working overtime?

25. Tell me about your proudest professional Utilization Review Nurse accomplishment.

26. Give me an Utilization Review Nurse example of a time you were able to be creative with your work. What was exciting or difficult about it?

27. This Utilization Review Nurse job requires a lot of stamina. How do you think you will be able to withstand these rigors?

28. How many Utilization Review Nurse hours did you spend dedicated to a task before you attained your current level of proficiency?

29. Describe a Utilization Review Nurse situation when you were able to have a positive influence on the actions

of others

30. What is your current Utilization Review Nurse life goal is and where do you want to end up?

31. When you look back in a year from now and I bump into you at our holiday Utilization Review Nurse party, how you will have known that working here was a good decision and what would you tell me?

32. What do you want to do?

33. Describe a time when you were confronted with an angry Utilization Review Nurse customer, supervisor or coworker. How did you react?

34. Tell us me about an important Utilization Review Nurse goal that you set in the past. Were you successful? Why?

35. Who is someone you aspire to be like, and why?

36. Are there specific times you cannot work?

37. Which one of the following three Utilization Review Nurse things motivates you most: sense of ownership, intellectual curiosity, or collaborating with peers?

38. What Utilization Review Nurse steps did you take to calm things down?

39. Have you ever filed for workers compensation?

40. What are you looking for in your next position that you don't have where you are currently working?

41. Tell me about a time when you had to deliver some unpleasant or sensitive Utilization Review Nurse information to someone. How did you handle the situation?

42. The school is the place you did most of your formal learning. What is it about the school and the Utilization Review Nurse way it is organised that encouraged you to attend?

43. Can you perform (any or all of the Utilization Review Nurse job functions) with or without accommodation?

44. If your Utilization Review Nurse memory was wiped and you had to read one book to regain your perspective, which would it be?

45. Can you think of products, ads, or brands that are anti-materialistic?

46. What would you do if you were given an assignment but no instruction on how to perform the duties involved?

47. What do you want to be known for?

48. Give an Utilization Review Nurse example of a time when you went above and beyond the call of duty

49. How do you handle stress?

50. Describe the Utilization Review Nurse task you had to accomplish. What were your responsibilities in this situation?

51. Over a several month Utilization Review Nurse period, you realize that a number of auto thefts have occurred in the parking lot. What type of actions might you consider to address the problem?

52. What motivates you to stay?

53. How would you define 'Utilization Review Nurse success' for someone in your chosen career?

54. There is a movement away from materialism in our Utilization Review Nurse culture. Can you think of products, ads, or brands that are anti-materialistic?

55. What is your greatest strength or Utilization Review Nurse weakness?

56. What is your personal Utilization Review Nurse mission, and how does this job description align with that Utilization Review Nurse mission?

57. In 2026, how do you envision Personal Utilization Review Nurse Data Fusion making you smarter?

58. What have you done to prepare yourself for today?

59. Give an Utilization Review Nurse example of a time when you had to be relatively quick in coming to a

decision. How did it turn out?

60. How can our Utilization Review Nurse company increase employee engagement and retain top performers?

61. Do you feel you make a Utilization Review Nurse difference?

62. Do you get ill from stress?

63. Tell me about a time you were dissatisfied in your work. What could have been done to make it better?

64. What obstacles did you encounter, and how did you overcome them?

65. In which aspects do you excel?

66. Would you be able and willing to work overtime as necessary?

67. Where were you born?

68. What do you do to cope with stress?

69. What were the easiest subjects in school for you?

70. What's your favorite thing about marketing? And why do you love it?

71. Finishing up your Junior summer, heading into your senior year, what were you thinking about plans for after graduation?

72. What child care arrangements have you made?

73. Do sources of thriving apply to your own Utilization Review Nurse life and work, or people you know?

Persuasion

1. Why should people believe you?

2. Have you ever had to persuade a Utilization Review Nurse group to accept a proposal or idea? How did you go about doing it? What was the result?

3. What will you learn?

4. In working with other Utilization Review Nurse team members, how might your preferences get in the way or block the success of the Utilization Review Nurse team?

5. Describe a Utilization Review Nurse situation in which you were able to positively influence the actions of others in a desired direction

6. Tell us about a time when you had to convince someone in authority about your Utilization Review Nurse ideas. How did it work out?

7. What Utilization Review Nurse questions could you raise that would get others to want to hire you?

8. Tell us about a time when you used Utilization Review Nurse facts and reason to persuade someone to accept your recommendation

9. Which actors and actresses are different from the Utilization Review Nurse way you envisioned them?

10. Describe a Utilization Review Nurse situation where you were able to use persuasion to successfully convince

someone to see things your way

11. Given your type, what about your preferences is likely to make you personally effective?

12. What do you believe you owe your family?

13. Tell us about a time when you used your Utilization Review Nurse leadership ability to gain support for what initially had strong opposition

14. What do the Utilization Review Nurse tasks look like from your point of view?

15. What would you consider to be a terrific place to go for a vacation?

16. On what matters in your Utilization Review Nurse life would you be open to family opinions or persuasion?

17. What are your primary Utilization Review Nurse personality preferences?

18. To what extent are Utilization Review Nurse education, economic stability, family background, temperament, race, religion, ethnicity, or language important to you?

19. How is your offer most persuasive?

20. Describe a time when you were able to convince a skeptical or resistant Utilization Review Nurse customer to purchase a project or utilize your services

21. Which lines, Utilization Review Nurse ideas, and/or

actions resonate with you or repulse you?

22. What do you know about the lives of women in the late 18th century?

23. Have you ever had to persuade a peer or Utilization Review Nurse manager to accept an idea that you knew they would not like? Describe the resistance you met and how you overcame it

24. How do you get a peer or Utilization Review Nurse colleague to accept one of your ideas?

25. Tell us about a time when you were able to successfully influence another person

26. You are telephoning somebody about something that is important to you. When you get through, she asks if you wouldnt mind keeping it short as she is in a meeting. Do you?

27. You are introduced to three new people and miss one of the names. What do you do?

28. Suppose you must implement an unpopular Utilization Review Nurse policy at work. You want to persuade your employees that the Utilization Review Nurse policy is a positive change. Should you present one side of the issue or both sides?

29. Advertise a Utilization Review Nurse movie. What elements would you emphasize to create print or radio campaigns?

30. In selling an Utilization Review Nurse idea, it is sometimes useful to use metaphors, analogies, or stories

to make your point. Give a recent example of when you were able to successfully do that

31. What elements would you emphasize to create print or radio campaigns?

32. Think about your Utilization Review Nurse character. What contemporary songs would you identify with?

33. What Utilization Review Nurse jobs are your primary preferences most often associated with?

34. Have you seen any reference to yourself on radio or TV or in the newspaper?

Personal Effectiveness

1. There are times when we are placed under extreme Utilization Review Nurse pressure on the job. Tell about a time when you were under such Utilization Review Nurse pressure and how you handled it

2. Keeping others informed of your progress/Utilization Review Nurse actions helps them fell comfortable. Tell your methods for keeping your supervisor advised of the status on projects

3. When you have been made aware of, or have discovered for yourself, a Utilization Review Nurse problem in your work performance, what was your course of action? Can you give an example?

4. It is important to maintain a positive Utilization Review Nurse attitude at work when you have other things on your mind. Give a specific example of when you were able to do that

5. Tell us about a time when your supervisor criticized your work. How did you respond?

6. Tell us about some demanding situations in which you managed to remain calm and composed

7. Give an Utilization Review Nurse example of a situation where others were intense but you were able to maintain your composure

8. Tell us about a recent Utilization Review Nurse job or experience that you would describe as a real learning experience? What did you learn from the Utilization Review Nurse job or experience?

9. What have you done to further your own professional Utilization Review Nurse development in the past 5 years

10. Tell us about a time when you took responsibility for an Utilization Review Nurse error and were held personally accountable

Basic interview question

1. Why should we hire you?

2. What can you do for us that other Utilization Review Nurse candidates can't?

3. What do you know about this Utilization Review Nurse industry?

4. When were you most satisfied in your Utilization Review Nurse job?

5. Where would you like to be in your Utilization Review Nurse career five years from now?

6. What's your ideal Utilization Review Nurse company?

7. Tell me about yourself.

8. What are your weaknesses?

9. What do you know about our Utilization Review Nurse company?

10. What were the responsibilities of your last position?

11. What did you like least about your last Utilization Review Nurse job?

12. What are your Utilization Review Nurse strengths?

13. Why are you leaving your present Utilization Review

Nurse job?

14. Do you have any Utilization Review Nurse questions for me?

15. Why do you want this Utilization Review Nurse job?

16. What attracted you to this Utilization Review Nurse company?

17. Behavioral Utilization Review Nurse interview questions

Strengths and Weaknesses

1. What's the hardest thing you've ever done?

2. Do you have a chip on your shoulder?

3. How will you contribute with your work and Utilization Review Nurse skills to make our company reach a specific revenue increase in 3 years?

4. In your professional Utilization Review Nurse career, what is the one thing you are most proud of, and likewise, what's the one thing you are least proud of?

5. Can you please describe a Utilization Review Nurse situation in which you had to overcome some serious obstacles or make some considerable sacrifices to achieve your goal?

6. How do you get out of your comfort zone in your Utilization Review Nurse life?

7. Why should I hire you vs the next person (or robot) to walk through the door?

8. Tell me about one of the more challenging Utilization Review Nurse projects you've done in your career. What was the goal, and how did you achieve it?

9. What are you good at, and what do you WANT to do?

10. Which superhero powers do you value most?

11. What do you want to be the best in the Utilization Review Nurse world at doing, and why do you want to be known for that?

12. What makes you lose track of time and want to work nonstop? Where do you find yourself in 'the flow'?

13. At our Utilization Review Nurse company, we believe we can do anything. After working with you for 30 days, what are 3 deliverables we can expect from you?

14. How would you do better?

15. What is the one Utilization Review Nurse word that best describes you?

16. Why shouldn't I hire you?

17. What are you most proud of?

18. If you wouldn't have learned the biggest Utilization Review Nurse lesson you have learned last year, how different your career would be today?

Delegation

1. Tell us how you go about delegating work?

2. What was the biggest mistake you have had when delegating work? The biggest Utilization Review Nurse success?

3. Do you consider yourself a macro or Utilization Review Nurse micro manager? How do you delegate?

4. How do you make the Utilization Review Nurse decision to delegate work?

Time Management Skills

1. Tell me about a time you set a Utilization Review Nurse goal for yourself. How did you go about ensuring that you would meet your objective?

2. Sometimes it's just not possible to get everything on your to-do list done. Tell me about a time your responsibilities got a little overwhelming. What did you do?

3. Describe a Utilization Review Nurse situation that required you to do a number of things at the same time. How did you handle it? What was the result?

4. Tell me about a time you had to be very strategic in order to meet all your top priorities.

5. Describe a long-Utilization Review Nurse term project that you managed. How did you keep everything moving along in a timely manner?

6. How do you determine priorities in scheduling your time? Give an Utilization Review Nurse example

7. How do you typically plan your Utilization Review Nurse day to manage your time effectively?

8. Give me an Utilization Review Nurse example of a time you managed numerous responsibilities. How did you handle that?

9. Of your current assignments, which do you consider to have required the greatest amount of Utilization Review Nurse effort with regard to planning/organization? How

have you accomplished this assignment? How would
you asses your effectiveness?

Most Common

1. Why are you interested in working for [insert Utilization Review Nurse company name here]?

2. If I called your Utilization Review Nurse boss right now and asked him what is an area that you could improve on, what would he say?

3. What was the hardest Utilization Review Nurse decision you have ever had to make?

4. Why Did You Switch Utilization Review Nurse Career Paths?

5. Do we have your Utilization Review Nurse permission to verify your employment eligibility and do employment/background checks?

6. What Utilization Review Nurse kind of work environment do you like best?

7. What value will you bring to the position?

8. How do you handle your Utilization Review Nurse calendar and schedule? What apps/systems do you use?

9. What do you expect to be doing in five Utilization Review Nurse years' time?

10. What's the Utilization Review Nurse job you want two Utilization Review Nurse jobs from now, and how does this role help you get there?

11. Are you a fast learner? How long will it take you to begin adding value?

12. What motivates you to deliver your greatest Utilization Review Nurse effort?

13. Tell me about the toughest Utilization Review Nurse decision you had to make in the last six months.

14. Why are you looking for a new Utilization Review Nurse job?

15. Where do you see yourself in 2 Utilization Review Nurse years time?

16. If you owned the Utilization Review Nurse company, what would you change?

17. Have you ever had to work with a person you didn't get along with? How did you handle the Utilization Review Nurse problem?

18. What Utilization Review Nurse challenges and opportunities do you think the company faces?

19. Were you involved in any Utilization Review Nurse teams or societies at university?

20. How many people do you think are online on Facebook in Chicago right now?

21. How well do you handle rejection?

22. What do you plan to do if...?

23. What do you think you will be doing in this Utilization Review Nurse role?

24. How long would you stay with us?

25. Can you show me Utilization Review Nurse proof of ROI (return on investment) on marketing campaign(s) that you've led, designed, or otherwise participated in, as well as what lessons, both good and bad, you learned from them?

26. What has been your greatest achievement?

27. Where else have you applied to?

28. Have you ever had to learn a Utilization Review Nurse skill and then apply it immediately?

29. Are you overqualified for this Utilization Review Nurse job?

30. Have you ever been in a Utilization Review Nurse situation where you disagreed with your manager? How did you resolve the disagreement?

31. What special qualifications and Utilization Review Nurse experiences do you have?

32. Discuss your resume.

33. How would you feel about re-locating?

34. Why do you want to work remotely?

35. What is your dream Utilization Review Nurse job? Describe it to me.

36. What Utilization Review Nurse questions do you have for us?

37. What is your experience with hiring and firing Utilization Review Nurse employees?

38. What was the biggest challenge you ever faced?

39. How would your worst enemy describe you?

40. What Would Be Something That Would Make our Utilization Review Nurse Company Hesitate and Not Hire You?

41. What has been the biggest disappointment in your Utilization Review Nurse life?

42. Where do you see yourself in five Utilization Review Nurse years? Ten Utilization Review Nurse years?

43. How would your last Utilization Review Nurse boss or your coworkers describe you?

44. What is your favorite Utilization Review Nurse website?

45. (If you have had interviews) Why do you think you haven't been offered a Utilization Review Nurse job yet?

46. What Was Your Greatest Professional Challenge and How Did You Cope?

47. How do you organize Utilization Review Nurse files, links, and tabs on your computer?

48. Why do you like to manage people?

49. Give us an Utilization Review Nurse example of a situation where you faced conflict or difficult communication problems

50. Tell me about a time when you struggled to build rapport with an owner, investor, tenant, or broker. What would you have done differently?

51. What will your referees say about you?

52. What were your objectives for last year? Did you achieve them?

53. What is the most difficult Utilization Review Nurse situation you have faced?

54. Why are you leaving your current brokerage?

55. How do you schedule your Utilization Review Nurse day?

56. Tell me about an Utilization Review Nurse accomplishment you are most proud of.

57. What do you find are the most difficult Utilization Review Nurse decisions to make?

58. Have you ever had a conflict with a Utilization Review Nurse boss or professor? How was it resolved?

59. When was the last time you were angry and what happened?

60. What are your Utilization Review Nurse career goals? How will you get there?

61. How would you describe the Utilization Review Nurse essence of success? According to your definition of success, how successful have you been so far?

62. Can you work under Utilization Review Nurse pressure?

63. Would you describe a Utilization Review Nurse situation in which your work was criticized?

64. Why do you want to work for this Utilization Review Nurse company?

65. Tell me about a time when you made a mistake at work? How did you go about rectifying it? What did you learn from the mistake?

66. Tell me about a time when you disagreed with your Utilization Review Nurse boss.

67. (If you have applied to lots of Utilization Review Nurse places) Why haven't you had many interviews?

68. What are your salary Utilization Review Nurse requirements? (Hint: if you're not sure what's a fair salary range and compensation package, research the job

title and/or company on Glassdoor.)

69. How long would it take you to make a meaningful Utilization Review Nurse contribution to our firm?

70. What do you know about this Utilization Review Nurse company?

71. How would you describe your own Utilization Review Nurse personality?

72. What are your aspirations beyond this Utilization Review Nurse job?

73. Are you willing to relocate?

74. How would you handle a Utilization Review Nurse team situation where Nina wants to dive right in, Joe is telecommuting, and Todd wants to gut the project?

75. How do you feel about becoming Utilization Review Nurse friends with your coworkers? Is it a good idea or a bad idea?

76. What is your dream Utilization Review Nurse job?

77. Why do you think you'd be the right administrative assistant for me/for this Utilization Review Nurse office?

78. What do you think of our Utilization Review Nurse competitors?

79. What is your biggest Utilization Review Nurse weakness?

80. As a Utilization Review Nurse manager in this role, you will be responsible for leading a team of X people. What specifically will you do during year one to help ensure they each become more valuable to the company and stronger performers overall?

81. How have you changed the Utilization Review Nurse nature of your job?

82. Are you prepared to relocate?

83. Why are you applying for this position?

84. Tell me about a time you made a mistake.

85. What was it about this Utilization Review Nurse job description that caught your eye?

86. How do you prepare for Utilization Review Nurse meetings and facilitate Utilization Review Nurse meetings? What do you make sure to do during a meeting?

87. What would you do for us? What can you do for us that someone else can't?

88. Why were you let go from your last position?

89. What important Utilization Review Nurse trends do you see in our industry?

90. Can you act on your own initiative?

91. If you could start your Utilization Review Nurse career again, what would you do differently?

92. How do you evaluate Utilization Review Nurse success?

93. Give us an Utilization Review Nurse example of a situation where you didn't meet your goals or objectives.

94. What Are Your Expectations Regarding Salary?

95. Why haven't you applied to more firms?

96. What would you say are your strong Utilization Review Nurse points?

97. You have not done this sort of Utilization Review Nurse job before. How will you succeed?

98. Would your current Utilization Review Nurse boss describe you as the type of person who goes that extra mile?

99. How much does your last Utilization Review Nurse job resemble the one you are applying for? What are the differences?

100. Where do you see yourself in 5 Utilization Review Nurse years? 10 Utilization Review Nurse years?

101. What new Utilization Review Nurse skills are you looking to develop this year?

102. Who are our Utilization Review Nurse competitors?

103. Do you prefer to work in a small, medium or large Utilization Review Nurse company?

104. Why are you looking to leave your current Utilization Review Nurse role?

105. Why should we give you this Utilization Review Nurse job?

106. What can you offer us that someone else can not?

107. What interests do you have outside work?

108. Tell me about a time you disagreed with a Utilization Review Nurse decision. What did you do?

109. What are your salary Utilization Review Nurse requirements or expectations?

110. Tell me about an important Utilization Review Nurse decision you had to make... how did you go about deciding?

111. What is your Utilization Review Nurse leadership style?

112. Describe a typical work week for you.

113. What do you look for when you hire people?

114. What Is Your Ideal Utilization Review Nurse Job?

115. If you had a Utilization Review Nurse problem when the rest of your remote team was offline, how would you go about solving it?

116. Are you a Utilization Review Nurse leader? (Utilization Review Nurse leadership)

117. How do you deal with adversity?

118. What is your Utilization Review Nurse management style?

119. What do you know about us - or - What do we do?

120. Have you ever ran an entrepreneurial Utilization Review Nurse business, even something as simple as selling collectible cards in high school?

121. What do you do when you are late for work?

122. Briefly walk me through your Utilization Review Nurse background and experience as it relates to our opening.

123. How would you evaluate your present firm?

124. Being an Utilization Review Nurse can be a stressful Utilization Review Nurse job. Tell me about a time when you had to multitask a deadline, a phone ringing

off the hook, and an error to fix all at the same time, or something similar to that. What did you prioritize on this crazy day and why?

125. Do you have any Utilization Review Nurse questions about the job or the company?

126. Are you a Utilization Review Nurse leader?

127. Are you willing to travel?

128. Are you a good Utilization Review Nurse manager? Give an example. Why do you feel you have top Utilization Review Nurse managerial potential?

129. What sort of salary are you looking for?

130. Tell me about using XYZ.

131. What can we expect from you in your first three months?

132. Why do you want to be a .... ?

133. What's your availability?

134. What do you like to do outside of work?

135. Tell me how you handled a difficult Utilization Review Nurse situation.

136. What do you see as the most difficult Utilization Review Nurse task in being a manager?

137. What are your Utilization Review Nurse future goals?

138. Do you have at least a few months worth of living expenses in the bank?

139. What blogs and Utilization Review Nurse resources do you follow online to keep up with the industry?

140. Why should I hire you vs the next person (or robot) to walk through the door?

141. What do you know about our Utilization Review Nurse company?

142. What Utilization Review Nurse questions haven't I asked you?

143. How would you deal with an angry or irate Utilization Review Nurse customer?

144. Why did you choose a Utilization Review Nurse career in …?

145. Tell me about the last time a co-worker or Utilization Review Nurse customer got angry with you. What happened?

146. What do you think of the last Utilization Review Nurse company you worked for?

147. If we hire you, how will you help grow your Utilization Review Nurse business (through our agency)?

148. Tell me about a special Utilization Review Nurse contribution you have made to your employer.

149. You walk into the Utilization Review Nurse office and have 8 emails and 4 voicemails from clients before your day has even started, all with different urgent requests. What do you do?

150. A snail is at the bottom of a 30-foot well. Each Utilization Review Nurse day he climbs up three feet, but at night he slips back two feet. How many Utilization Review Nurse days will it take him to climb out of the well?

151. What is a Utilization Review Nurse quarter of a half?

152. How would you explain a 10% departmental salary cut and still retain Utilization Review Nurse loyalty?

153. Your first year in this Utilization Review Nurse industry can be very tough. Would you be willing to become a junior agent and join a team?

154. What drives you to achieve your objectives?

155. What did you earn in your last Utilization Review Nurse job? What level of salary are you looking for now?

156. What do your work colleagues think of you?

157. Why do you want to work for _____?

158. What Utilization Review Nurse questions do you have for me?

159. What Are Your Professional Weaknesses?

160. Did you feel you progressed satisfactorily in your last Utilization Review Nurse job?

161. Do you enjoy travelling?

162. What would you do if one of our Utilization Review Nurse competitors offered you a position?

163. Which lead Utilization Review Nurse generation source did you see the best ROI from?

164. How much do you expect if we offer this position to you?

165. Give a time when you went above and beyond the Utilization Review Nurse requirements for a project.

166. Why Is There A Utilization Review Nurse Gap In Your Employment?

167. How would you deconstruct a mobile phone? Explain it to me like I had never seen it before.

168. What was the most difficult Utilization Review Nurse decision you ever had to make?

169. Tell us about a time when you felt that conflict or differences were a positive driving force in your Utilization Review Nurse organization. How did handle

the conflict to optimise its benefit?

170. How many people did you supervise on your last Utilization Review Nurse job?

171. How many Utilization Review Nurse hours are you prepared to work?

172. Why Do You Want To Work For Our Utilization Review Nurse Company?

173. How did you end up in the administrative field?

174. In what Utilization Review Nurse kind of a work environment are you most comfortable?

175. Who was your best Utilization Review Nurse boss and who was the worst?

176. What Is Your Greatest Professional Achievement To Date?

177. If you made it all the Utilization Review Nurse way to the end of this guide, bravo! What did we miss here in our best interview questions guide? Do you have a favorite interview question you like to ask? What is it?

178. Do you have any Utilization Review Nurse questions or concerns about your ability to do the job?

179. How do you go about solving Utilization Review Nurse problems?

180. What are your biggest Utilization Review Nurse strengths?

181. Why do you think Utilization Review Nurse graduates in .. [your degree subject] .. would be good at .. [job role you have applied for] .. ?

182. What is your most valuable asset when it comes to remote work?

183. What are your hobbies?

184. Describe the last significant conflict you had at work and how you handled it?

185. What gets your fired up and leaping out of bed in the morning?

186. What would your direct reports say about you?

187. What would your current Utilization Review Nurse manager say are your strengths?

188. What would you look to accomplish in the first 30 days/60 days/90 days on the Utilization Review Nurse job?

189. What do you do when you sense a project is going to take longer than expected?

190. Describe your approach to Utilization Review Nurse problem-solving?

191. What is the toughest part of a Utilization Review Nurse job for you?

192. Do You Have Any Utilization Review Nurse Questions For Us?

193. How do you handle Utilization Review Nurse pressure?

194. What do you like to do in your spare time?

195. How Would Your Co-Workers/Managers Describe You?

196. What really drives Utilization Review Nurse results in this job?

197. Did you enjoy Utilization Review Nurse university?

198. Why did you choose this particular Utilization Review Nurse career path?

199. Tell me how you think other people would describe you.

200. Did you ever fire anyone? If so, what were the Utilization Review Nurse reasons and how did you handle it?

201. Where do you see yourself in 5 Utilization Review Nurse years?

202. What are three Utilization Review Nurse things most important to you in a job?

203. What Utilization Review Nurse challenges are you looking for in this position?

204. Do you prefer Utilization Review Nurse staff or line work? Why?

205. What are your Utilization Review Nurse career goals?

206. How do you see this position assisting you in achieving your Utilization Review Nurse career goals?

207. How do you use Utilization Review Nurse technology throughout the day, in your job and for pleasure?

208. Tell me what you liked best and least about working at ABC.

209. Did your level of responsibility grow or change while you were at ABC?

210. Have you ever worked in a Utilization Review Nurse situation when there was no processes or procedures in place?

211. What was your biggest mistake as a new Utilization Review Nurse agent? Have you overcome it? How?

212. How do you handle criticism?

213. Tell me a little about yourself.

214. What was the last Utilization Review Nurse book you've read for fun?

215. Would you work 40+ Utilization Review Nurse hours a week?

216. What is your superpower?

217. What was your biggest setback?

218. What will you do if you don't get this position?

219. What are your computing Utilization Review Nurse skills like?

220. If you know your Utilization Review Nurse boss is 100% wrong about something, how would you handle this?

221. Would you have a Utilization Review Nurse problem cleaning the toilets?

222. How would you fire someone?

223. How have you helped increase Utilization Review Nurse sales? Profits?

224. Why was there a Utilization Review Nurse gap in your employment between [insert date] and [insert date]?

225. Why would you want a position like this?

226. What is your biggest Utilization Review Nurse weakness as a manager?

227. Have you ever been on a Utilization Review Nurse team where someone was not pulling their own weight?

How did you handle it?

228. How many transaction Utilization Review Nurse sides did you close this year?

229. Have you ever been in a difficult Utilization Review Nurse situation when you needed to remain positive? How did you handle it?

230. If a client emailed you asking for something outside of your territory at the Utilization Review Nurse company, how would you handle it?

231. Let's get specific. Tell me about your Utilization Review Nurse job at Company ABC.

232. What other careers have you considered/applied for?

233. Why do you want to work for our Utilization Review Nurse company in this role?

234. What Utilization Review Nurse environments allow you to be especially effective?

235. What are your salary Utilization Review Nurse requirements?

236. Tell me about a time when you were happiest at work. Why did you feel that Utilization Review Nurse way?

237. What would your first 30, 60, and 90 Utilization Review Nurse day plans look like in this role?

238. What Utilization Review Nurse kind of salary are

you worth?

239. If I called your Utilization Review Nurse boss right now and asked him/her what is an area that you could improve on, what would he/she say?

240. Why do you think you would like working for us?

241. Do you like working with figures more than Utilization Review Nurse words?

242. How would you handle Utilization Review Nurse lack of face-to-face contact when you work remotely?

243. What is your ideal work schedule in regards to flex-time and in-Utilization Review Nurse office and remote working?

244. What interests you about this Utilization Review Nurse job?

245. Can you work under pressures, deadlines, etc.?

246. Why did you choose your Utilization Review Nurse university and what factors influenced your choice?

247. What were your Utilization Review Nurse bosses' strengths/weaknesses?

248. Where do you see yourself in 3 , 5, 10 Utilization Review Nurse years time?

249. What are some of your Utilization Review Nurse leadership experiences?

250. How did you hear about this position?

251. What motivates you?

252. What did you like, dislike about your last Utilization Review Nurse job?

253. Discuss your educational Utilization Review Nurse background.

254. How do you utilize the Internet, video tours, and social media to sell property or homes?

255. What are three Utilization Review Nurse things your former manager would like you to improve on?

256. What are your biggest accomplishments?

257. What are you most proud of?

258. What did you like best and least in your last position?

259. How did you build up your own personal social media channels and online presence? What do you think works or does not work?

260. Why did you choose your Utilization Review Nurse degree subject?

261. If you could relive the last 10 Utilization Review Nurse years of your life.

262. Where else have you interviewed at?

263. What would you say are your weak Utilization Review Nurse points?

264. What does "working remotely" actually look like for you?

265. Do you feel you might be better off in a different size Utilization Review Nurse company? Different type Utilization Review Nurse company?

266. In your present position, what Utilization Review Nurse problems have you identified that had previously been overlooked?

267. Would you work Utilization Review Nurse holidays/weekends?

268. Tell me about your salary expectations.

269. What are your Utilization Review Nurse strengths and weaknesses?

270. Tell me about a time when you had to give someone difficult Utilization Review Nurse feedback. How did you handle it?

271. Why have you made so many Utilization Review Nurse applications?

272. Where Do You See Yourself in 5/10/20 Utilization Review Nurse Years?

273. We're considering two other Utilization Review

Nurse candidates for this position. Why should we hire you rather than someone else?

274. How do you take Utilization Review Nurse direction?

275. How quickly will we see Utilization Review Nurse results from hiring you? Would you stake your job on achieving that result by a certain date?

276. How would you manage a project with a lot of Utilization Review Nurse steps and a lot of people?

277. What other Utilization Review Nurse types of jobs or companies are you considering?

278. (If you have been offered a Utilization Review Nurse job) Are you going to take the Utilization Review Nurse job?

279. Describe yourself.

280. What draws you to this Utilization Review Nurse industry?

281. Tell me about your Utilization Review Nurse skills in (insert crucial skill for the role). How many years experience do you have in it and how would you rate yourself on a 1-10 scale, with 10 being an expert?

282. Why haven't you found a new position before now?

283. What do you consider to be your biggest

professional achievement?

284. What is the name of our CEO?

285. How has your Utilization Review Nurse education prepared you for your career?

286. When I speak to your last [or present] Utilization Review Nurse boss, what is he or she going to say about you?

287. Are you creative?

288. In your current or last position, what are or were your five most significant accomplishments?

289. What Are You Looking For In This Utilization Review Nurse Job?

290. What do you look for in a Utilization Review Nurse job?

291. What are the major Utilization Review Nurse reasons for your success?

292. What do you like and dislike about the Utilization Review Nurse job we are discussing?

293. How many Utilization Review Nurse applications have you made?

294. Would you describe yourself as competitive?

295. What scares you the most in Utilization Review Nurse life?

296. Tell me about a time when you demonstrated Utilization Review Nurse leadership and initiative?

297. How would you weigh an airplane, like a Boeing 747, without a scale?

298. Do you generally speak to people before they speak to you?

299. Give me Utilization Review Nurse proof of your persuasiveness.

300. How do you process Utilization Review Nurse information??

301. How much Utilization Review Nurse money did you account for?

302. How do you balance your work Utilization Review Nurse life and the rest of your Utilization Review Nurse life?

303. What do you think of your Utilization Review Nurse boss?

304. When did you depart from the Utilization Review Nurse party line to accomplish your goal?

305. What was the worst Utilization Review Nurse day you've ever had at work and why?

306. Where do you see yourself in five Utilization Review Nurse years?

307. What would your ideal Utilization Review Nurse job be?

308. Do you like working in a Utilization Review Nurse team environment or do you prefer working alone?

309. What do you like the most and least about working in this Utilization Review Nurse industry?

310. What are your biggest weaknesses?

311. How do you use different Utilization Review Nurse communication tools in different situations?

312. Are you a Utilization Review Nurse leader or a follower?

313. What is the single most important Utilization Review Nurse factor that would make you happy in your job that is not from the job itself?

314. Do you prefer working in a Utilization Review Nurse team or on your own?

315. Tell me about a time when you had to deal with an irate Utilization Review Nurse customer. How did you handle the situation?

316. Before you came in, I looked at the Utilization Review Nurse mission and vision from your current (or past) company. What is it in your own words?

317. If you were to rank them, what are the three traits your top performers have in common?

318. Are there any Utilization Review Nurse tasks or jobs you feel are beneath you?

319. What about the Utilization Review Nurse job offered do you find the most attractive? Least attractive?

320. Why do you want to leave your current Utilization Review Nurse company?

321. What do your subordinates think of you?

322. How would you describe the Utilization Review Nurse pace at which you work?

323. What are you looking for in your next Utilization Review Nurse job? What is important to you?

324. How much are you looking for?

325. How do you prioritize Utilization Review Nurse tasks?

326. Out of all the other Utilization Review Nurse candidates, why should we hire you?

327. What was your salary in your last Utilization Review Nurse job?

328. What Utilization Review Nurse percentage of employees was brought in by current employees?

329. What are your co-worker pet peeves?

330. Who's your Utilization Review Nurse mentor?

331. How do you deal with a project that's gone over Utilization Review Nurse budget or pushed past the deadline?

332. How would you feel about frequent travel?

333. What gets you up in the morning?

334. If I Utilization Review Nurse spoke with your previous boss, what would he say are your greatest strengths and weaknesses?

335. How much do you know about our Utilization Review Nurse company, products and services?

336. Name one person, alive or dead, that you would want to meet and why?

337. I checked out your last company's social media accounts to see what your marketing department has been up to. What did you think of their current campaign?

338. Tell me about a time when you took a risk... How did you handle it?

339. What makes you uncomfortable?

340. Tell me about at least one significant Utilization Review Nurse career achievement.

341. Why do you want to work for us?

342. Do you work best independently or as part of a Utilization Review Nurse team?

343. What gets you out of bed in the morning?

344. What Is Your Favoured Work Utilization Review Nurse Environment?

345. What are the company's highest-priority Utilization Review Nurse goals this year, and how would my role contribute?

346. Describe your ideal Utilization Review Nurse job?

347. How did you learn about the opening?

348. What Do You Do For Utilization Review Nurse Fun?

349. What do you need in your physical Utilization Review Nurse workspace to be successful in your job?

350. Give us an Utilization Review Nurse example of when you have worked to an unreasonable deadline or been faced with a huge challenge.

351. What Are Your Professional Utilization Review Nurse Strengths?

352. Have you helped reduce costs? How?

353. Why Do You Want To Work At [Utilization Review Nurse Company Name]?

354. In your current or last position, what Utilization Review Nurse features did you like the most? Least?

355. How do you plan to achieve those Utilization Review Nurse goals?

356. I'm not sure you're the perfect fit. Why do you think you'd be a great Utilization Review Nurse candidate?

357. Why Are You Leaving Your Current Utilization Review Nurse Job?

358. Do You Have Interviews With Other Utilization Review Nurse Companies?

359. What do you expect me to accomplish in the first 90 days?

360. Why do you think this Utilization Review Nurse industry would sustain your interest in the long haul?

361. Tell me about a time when you Utilization Review Nurse planned and arranged a large project or event? What steps did you take?

362. How do you feel about leaving all of your Utilization Review Nurse benefits?

363. Why do you want to work as a real Utilization Review Nurse estate agent?

364. Do you have an established farm Utilization Review

Nurse area? Are you planning on staying there?

365. Can You Tell Me About Yourself?

366. Tell me about a time when you worked as part of a Utilization Review Nurse team? How did you handle it?

367. How would you describe yourself?

368. What was the last Utilization Review Nurse book you read? Movie you saw? Sporting event you attended?

369. What are your pet peeves?

370. Tell me about the best Utilization Review Nurse boss you ever had. Why did you enjoy working for them so much?

371. I used to work with (insert name of professional Utilization Review Nurse contact) at your former company. Did you ever meet him while you were working there?

372. What about this Utilization Review Nurse job do you find exciting?

373. What would your current Utilization Review Nurse manager say are your weaknesses?

374. What two or three Utilization Review Nurse things would be most important to you in your ideal job, and why?

375. What are you looking to gain out of associating with our brokerage?

376. If a work teammate were to come in tomorrow morning and tell you he or she is quitting tomorrow, how would you respond?

377. Had you thought of leaving your present position before? If so, what do you think held you there?

378. What is the first thing you would change, if you were to start work here?

379. Wow, (insert Utilization Review Nurse company name from their resume) is an impressive Utilization Review Nurse company, but I've heard their culture is a bit (insert adjective that you know of Utilization Review Nurse company culture). How did you find you fit into that culture?

380. What Utilization Review Nurse career options do you have at the moment?

381. What do you find most challenging when you accompany prospective Utilization Review Nurse clients on showings? Why?

382. Why are you leaving (did you leave) ABC?

383. What's your biggest concern about working remotely?

384. Describe your dream Utilization Review Nurse job.

385. If you were an animal, which one would you want to be?

386. Why do you want to leave your current Utilization Review Nurse job?

387. Tell me about a time you had someone on your Utilization Review Nurse team who was an incredible challenge. What did you do to manage them, and how did the situation turn out?

388. How do you resolve conflict on a project Utilization Review Nurse team?

Adaptability

1. When the unexpected happens what next?

2. How can a hobby prepare you for work?

3. Tell us about a Utilization Review Nurse situation in which you had to adjust to changes over which you had no control. How did you handle it?

4. What Utilization Review Nurse benefits do you get from belonging to this organization?

5. How do you know if an Utilization Review Nurse organization is adaptable?

6. Describe a major change that occurred in a Utilization Review Nurse job that you held. How did you adapt to this change?

7. What is your biggest work related Utilization Review Nurse failure in the last six months and how did you overcome it?

8. What is meant by being more flexible?

9. What Utilization Review Nurse skills, activities and attitudes lead to promotion?

10. What Utilization Review Nurse role should a hobby play in this job interview?

11. What was your biggest Utilization Review Nurse failure?

12. What's your biggest Utilization Review Nurse failure

- why is it a Utilization Review Nurse failure and what did you learn from it?

13. Tell me about a time you were under a lot of Utilization Review Nurse pressure. What was going on and how did you get through it?

14. Give me an Utilization Review Nurse example of a time when you had to think on your feet in order to delicately extricate yourself from a difficult or awkward situation.

15. What Utilization Review Nurse kinds of educational decisions make you more promotable?

16. What professional organizations support your careers of interest?

17. How do different project Utilization Review Nurse types, procurement routes, clients, and / or locations influence your pull?

18. Tell us about a time that you had to adapt to a difficult Utilization Review Nurse situation

19. What careers would allow you to do what you really enjoy doing?

20. In what Utilization Review Nurse ways can you build on your present skills?

21. How does one design for time?

22. What s the long-Utilization Review Nurse term plan beyond your first job at our company?

23. How do we foster a Utilization Review Nurse culture that allows open dialog between everyone regardless of rank?

24. What ongoing professional Utilization Review Nurse development opportunities exist in this career?

25. How must you adapt in your workplace in order to advance?

26. How would you create and then lead an Utilization Review Nurse organization where the infrastructure is flexible, but yet efficient, effective, and reliable?

27. Describe a time when your Utilization Review Nurse team or company was undergoing some change. How did that impact you, and how did you adapt?

28. What do you do when priorities change quickly? Give one Utilization Review Nurse example of when this happened

29. What other occupations also require your Utilization Review Nurse skills?

30. When does a hobby start to become work?

31. How many times have you failed?

32. Tell me about a time when you failed. Why did it happen? What did you do next and what would you do differently if given another chance?

33. Tell me about the first Utilization Review Nurse job you've ever had. What did you do to learn the ropes?

34. At what point do you engage/ step away?

35. What is your greatest Utilization Review Nurse failure, and what did you learn from it?

36. How do Utilization Review Nurse leaders develop organizations capable of adapting in the volatile, uncertain, complex, and ambiguous environment envisioned by senior Utilization Review Nurse leaders?

37. If you do your Utilization Review Nurse job well, will you automatically get promoted?

38. Do you have enough stress to make you ill?

39. What is the meaning of Adaptability in the Utilization Review Nurse industry?

40. What is your biggest Utilization Review Nurse career screw-up?

41. Are you a resilient survivor?

42. How might a lateral move help you get the promotion?

43. Is ours a learning Utilization Review Nurse organization?

44. Describe a time when you failed to engage at the right level in your Utilization Review Nurse organization. Why did you do that and how did you handle the situation?

45. What are the licensing, certifications, and credentialing Utilization Review Nurse requirements for this job?

46. Tell me about two memorable Utilization Review Nurse projects, one success and one failure. To what do you attribute the success and failure?

47. Tell me about a time you failed. How did you deal with this Utilization Review Nurse situation?

48. In your chosen work Utilization Review Nurse area, what are five careers that seem attractive to you?

Planning and Organization

1. What do you do when your time schedule or project plan is upset by unforeseen circumstances? Give an Utilization Review Nurse example

2. What have you done in order to be effective with your Utilization Review Nurse organization and planning?

3. Describe how you develop a project team's Utilization Review Nurse goals and project plan?

4. How do you schedule your time? Set priorities? How do you handle doing twenty Utilization Review Nurse things at once?

5. Tell us about a time when you organized or Utilization Review Nurse planned an event that was very successful

Setting Goals

1. What Utilization Review Nurse company plans have you developed? Which ones have you reached? How did you reach them? Which have you missed? Why did you miss them?

2. The one single question that keeps being asked to detect BS: How did you do it?

3. Did you have a strategic plan? How was it developed? How did you communicate it to the rest of your Utilization Review Nurse staff?

4. What is something that you accomplished in the last 2 Utilization Review Nurse years that required a high amount of grit?

5. How do you communicate Utilization Review Nurse goals to subordinates? Give an example

6. What Utilization Review Nurse goals did you miss? Why did you miss them?

7. What Utilization Review Nurse goals have you met? What did you do to meet them?

8. What were your annual Utilization Review Nurse goals at your most current employer? How did you develop these Utilization Review Nurse goals?

9. What were your long-Utilization Review Nurse range plans at your most recent employer? What was your role in developing them?

10. How do you involve people in developing your unit's

Utilization Review Nurse goals? Give an example

More questions about you

1. How do you think I rate as an interviewer?

2. Was there a person in your Utilization Review Nurse career who really made a difference?

3. What is your favorite Utilization Review Nurse memory from childhood?

4. What do you look for in Utilization Review Nurse terms of culture—structured or entrepreneurial?

5. What do you ultimately want to become?

6. What do you like to do?

7. List five Utilization Review Nurse words that describe your character.

8. What Utilization Review Nurse kind of car do you drive?

9. How do you feel about taking no for an answer?

10. Who are your Utilization Review Nurse heroes?

11. What are you most proud of?

12. What are your lifelong Utilization Review Nurse dreams?

13. What is your greatest achievement outside of work?

14. Tell me one thing about yourself you wouldn't want me to know.

15. What three Utilization Review Nurse character traits would your friends use to describe you?

16. What is your personal Utilization Review Nurse mission statement?

17. What Utilization Review Nurse techniques and tools do you use to keep yourself organized?

18. What do you like to do for Utilization Review Nurse fun?

19. What are three positive Utilization Review Nurse character traits you don't have?

20. What do you do in your spare time?

21. What's the best Utilization Review Nurse movie you've seen in the last year?

22. How would you feel about working for someone who knows less than you?

23. What's the most important thing you learned in school?

24. What would you do if you won the lottery?

25. Who was your favorite Utilization Review Nurse manager and why?

26. Give Utilization Review Nurse examples of ideas you've had or implemented.

27. What would be your ideal working Utilization Review Nurse environment?

28. If you had to choose one, would you consider yourself a big-Utilization Review Nurse picture person or a detail-oriented person?

29. What magazines do you subscribe to?

30. There's no right or wrong answer, but if you could be anywhere in the Utilization Review Nurse world right now, where would you be?

31. What will you miss about your present/last Utilization Review Nurse job?

32. Why did you choose your major?

33. Tell me the Utilization Review Nurse difference between good and exceptional.

34. What Utilization Review Nurse kind of personality do you work best with and why?

35. What is your greatest fear?

36. How would you describe your work Utilization Review Nurse style?

37. Who has impacted you most in your Utilization Review Nurse career and how?

38. What negative thing would your last Utilization

Review Nurse boss say about you?

39. What's the last Utilization Review Nurse book you read?

40. What is your biggest regret and why?

41. Do you think a Utilization Review Nurse leader should be feared or liked?

42. What do you think of your previous Utilization Review Nurse boss?

43. Tell me about your proudest achievement.

44. What are three positive Utilization Review Nurse things your last boss would say about you?

45. If you were interviewing someone for this position, what traits would you look for?

46. What are the Utilization Review Nurse qualities of a good leader? A bad leader?

Detail-Oriented

1. Describe a Utilization Review Nurse situation where you had the option to leave the details to others or you could take care of them yourself

2. Tell us about a Utilization Review Nurse situation where attention to detail was either important or unimportant in accomplishing an assigned task

3. Tell us about a difficult experience you had in working with Utilization Review Nurse details

4. Have the Utilization Review Nurse jobs you held in the past required little attention, moderate attention, or a great deal of attention to detail? Give me an example of a situation that illustrates this requirement

5. Do you prefer to work with the 'big Utilization Review Nurse picture' or the 'details' of a situation? Give me an example of an experience that illustrates your preference?

Culture Fit

1. If you were starting a Utilization Review Nurse company from scratch, what would you want your Utilization Review Nurse company's culture to be?

2. What would you fire a person for?

3. What keeps you awake at night?

4. Let's suppose that you found your dream Utilization Review Nurse job with your ideal company that pays you well and has a great career path, title, benefits and perks. You have to start in 2 days and all you have to do is tell your boss what you'd want to do at this dream Utilization Review Nurse job and you can have it - just like that. What would you say that you'd like to do?

5. What other commitments do you have in your Utilization Review Nurse life ... i.e. other jobs, school, family, community?

6. Why do you want to work for a startup when you could get a Utilization Review Nurse job at a larger company, make more money and have a better work/life balance?

7. What does your ideal work Utilization Review Nurse day look like?

8. What do you want from working with us? How can we help you accomplish that in this Utilization Review Nurse role?

9. In your Utilization Review Nurse opinion, what is leadership?

10. What are you passionate about outside of work?

11. What Utilization Review Nurse environment do you thrive in the most and what drives your passion?

12. What are your personal Utilization Review Nurse values? And if you believe that your personal Utilization Review Nurse values are aligned with the company's Utilization Review Nurse values, please describe why.

13. Are you the type to check your inbox on vacation?

14. Pick two of our Utilization Review Nurse company cultural values and provide an example for each where you've exemplified the value, preferably from your previous employment.

15. What do you see as your biggest Utilization Review Nurse contribution to the world in 30 years?

16. Fast, Good, and Cheap. Which two would you pick?

17. What does Utilization Review Nurse culture mean to you?

18. Consider three Utilization Review Nurse things – Humility, Hunger and Smarts. You may relate to one or all of these. Please tell me what you are the 'most-of' and

what you are the 'least-of'?

19. What specifically would you contribute to us during your first week of employment?

20. Are you incredibly passionate about solving the Utilization Review Nurse problem that we are solving. Do you dream about it? Do you spend free time on it?

21. Do Utilization Review Nurse heroes make moments or do moments make Utilization Review Nurse heroes?

Customer Orientation

1. How do you go about establishing rapport with a Utilization Review Nurse customer? What have you done to gain their confidence? Give an example

2. How do you handle Utilization Review Nurse problems with customers? Give an example

3. What have you done to improve Utilization Review Nurse relations with your customers?

Analytical Thinking

1. Tell us about your experience in past Utilization Review Nurse jobs that required you to be especially alert to details while doing the task involved

2. Give me a specific Utilization Review Nurse example of a time when you used good judgment and logic in solving a problem

3. In your current Utilization Review Nurse job role, what energizes you?

4. What do you think Tom Peters means when he says, If you have gone a whole week without being disobedient, you are doing yourself and your Utilization Review Nurse organization a disservice?

5. Tell us about a Utilization Review Nurse job or setting where great precision to detail was required to complete a task. How did you handle that situation?

6. Do you know what the Utilization Review Nurse outcome should be after you follow instructions?

7. What is your approach to solving Utilization Review Nurse problems?

8. Which of our Managerial Competencies most support your personal Utilization Review Nurse development goals?

9. Tell us about a time when you had to analyze Utilization Review Nurse information and make a recommendation. What kind of thought process did

you go through? What was your reasoning behind your decision?

10. Do you agree with author James Fixx, who asserts, In solving puzzles, a self-assured Utilization Review Nurse attitude is half the battle?

11. Do you ask yourself after every interaction with the Utilization Review Nurse team, Have I left them feeling stronger and more capable than before?

12. What is critical thinking and analytical thinking?

13. What rules do you feel should be changed?

14. How can we maximize the investment in your training, after the training?

15. What Utilization Review Nurse techniques do you know of to stimulate free association or brainstorming?

16. What is the greatest Utilization Review Nurse contribution you can make to this organization?

17. What's the connection between hands and the ocean?

18. How does this activity we're doing right now relate to thinking?

19. Give me an Utilization Review Nurse example of when you took a risk to achieve a goal. What was the outcome?

20. What are you looking at that no one else can see?

21. What happens when you are called upon to make a statement on the spot, to make a Utilization Review Nurse decision without having all the facts, to solve a problem that will only be exacerbated by delay?

22. What is your evaluation of the educational training at secondary level in our country?

23. What Utilization Review Nurse resources, human and other, remain untapped in our organization?

24. Should spent nuclear fuel be reprocessed?

25. Developing and using a detailed Utilization Review Nurse procedure is often very important in a job. Tell about a time when you needed to develop and use a detailed Utilization Review Nurse procedure to successfully complete a project

26. Ever see the face of someone you know in a potato chip?

27. Relate a specific Utilization Review Nurse instance when you found it necessary to be precise in your in order to complete the job

28. How does this activity we're doing right now relate to learning?

29. Describe the project or Utilization Review Nurse

situation which best demonstrates your analytical abilities. What was your role?

30. How did you go about making the changes (step by step)? Answer in Utilization Review Nurse depth or detail such as 'What were you thinking at that point?' or 'Tell me more about meeting with that person', or 'Lead me through your decision process'

31. What do you do when the patterns break down?

Stress Management

1. What was the most stressful Utilization Review Nurse situation you have faced? How did you deal with it?

2. How did you react when faced with constant time Utilization Review Nurse pressure? Give an example

3. People react differently when Utilization Review Nurse job demands are constantly changing; how do you react?

4. What Utilization Review Nurse kind of events cause you stress on the job?

Story

1. How did an Utilization Review Nurse action plan help you tackle your work?

2. What are the aspects of your community that makes promoting healthy weight and Utilization Review Nurse development in children particularly important, challenging or unique?

3. Tell me about three major Utilization Review Nurse life decisions that had you arrive here.

4. What do you suppose you found?

5. What can others take away and learn from your Utilization Review Nurse story?

6. What would you tell a friend about today?

7. Can you tell me the Utilization Review Nurse story of your prior success, challenges, and major responsibilities?

8. Identify Utilization Review Nurse examples from your past experience where you demonstrated those skills. How can you tell a story about your use of particular skills or knowledge?

9. How do you reach your imaginary Utilization Review Nurse world?

10. What Utilization Review Nurse background information do you need to know to understand your story?

11. What's your Utilization Review Nurse story?

12. Tell me where you're from.

13. Which of your personal Utilization Review Nurse experiences or memories is affecting your perceptions of the stories you tell?

14. Who do you want to be?

15. What is Your Experience with Work?

16. What barriers did you facd and how did you overcome them?

17. Whats your salary Utilization Review Nurse history?

18. How long have you been engaged in this process?

19. Who are your Utilization Review Nurse key partners?

20. Where did you work?

21. Have you ever been hurt at work, or do you know someone who was?

22. What are your next Utilization Review Nurse steps?

23. How can you tell a Utilization Review Nurse story about your use of particular skills or knowledge?

24. Tell me about a time when you were working on a Utilization Review Nurse team and you disagreed with someone about how to do something. Tell me the whole story and how it was resolved.

25. Did you feel you could tell your Utilization Review Nurse story fully?

26. How has your birth order made you who you are?

27. What restrictions do you have?

28. Will you play a game when you see it ?

29. What advice do you have for us?

30. How do you manage to escape?

31. What would you share with your family about what you learned here today?

32. Tell the Utilization Review Nurse story of how you reached your conclusion in you most recent problem solving (steps you took, who was involved, whom you consulted, the level of time and effort involved)?

Initiative

1. Give me Utilization Review Nurse examples of projects/tasks you started on your own

2. What Utilization Review Nurse sorts of things did you do at school that were beyond expectations?

3. Give me an Utilization Review Nurse example of when you had to go above and beyond the call of duty in order to get a job done

4. What changes did you develop at your most recent employer?

5. What Utilization Review Nurse kinds of things really get your excited?

6. Give some Utilization Review Nurse instances in which you anticipated problems and were able to influence a new direction

7. What Utilization Review Nurse sorts of projects did you generate that required you to go beyond your job description?

8. How did you get work assignments at your most recent employer?

Reference

1. Who are your mentors and why?

2. Can you provide 2-3 Utilization Review Nurse references that we could shoot a quick email to that would be ok sharing their experiences of working with you?

3. If I talked to your current/past Utilization Review Nurse manager and asked them to describe you, what would they say?

4. How do you and X know each other?

Brainteasers

1. Name as many uses as you can for a lemon.

2. How many gallons of paint does it take to paint the outside of the White House?

3. Why is a tennis ball fuzzy?

4. How many times heavier than a goldfish is a blue whale?

5. How many petrol stations are there in the UK?

6. How can you add eight eights to reach 1000?

7. How would you test a calculator?

8. Tell me 10 Utilization Review Nurse ways to use a pencil other than writing.

9. A windowless room has three light bulbs. You are outside the room with three switches, each controlling one of the light bulbs. If you can only enter the room one time, how can you determine which switch controls which light bulb?

10. Why is there fuzz on a tennis ball?

11. How many cows are in Canada?

12. How would you unload a 747 full of potatoes?

13. How can you tell if the light inside your refrigerator

is on or not?

14. Describe the color yellow to a blind person.

15. How would you weigh a plane without scales?

16. How many square feet of pizza are eaten in the United States each month?

17. If you were an animal, which one would you want to be?

18. How many gas stations are there in the U.S.?

19. How many times do a clock's hands overlap in a Utilization Review Nurse day?

20. Sell me this pencil.

21. If I roll two dice, what is the probability the sum of the amounts is nine?

22. Here's a mobile phone. Deconstruct it for me.

23. How many ping pong balls could fit in a Boeing 747?

24. What colour is your Utilization Review Nurse brain?

25. How many quarters (placed one on top of the other) would it take to reach the top of the Empire State Building?

26. How many golf balls can you fit in a car?

27. If you could be any animal, which one would you choose?

28. If you were a pizza delivery man, how would you benefit from scissors?

29. Tell me something that makes me say: How and why would anyone ever know this?

30. How many gallons of white house paint are sold in the United States each year?

31. How many times heavier than a mouse is an elephant?

32. What is the sum of the numbers one to 100?

33. Two mothers and two daughters sit down to eat eggs for breakfast. They ate three eggs and each person at the table ate an egg. Explain how.

34. You are shrunk to the height of a nickel and thrown into a blender. Your mass is reduced so that your density is the same as usual. The blades start moving in 60 seconds. What do you do?

35. What is your favorite Utilization Review Nurse song? Perform it for us now.

36. You just got back from a 2 week vacation and have 300 emails to process in the next hour. Go.

37. How would you move Mount Fuji?

38. Bring an Utilization Review Nurse item with you to the interview that best represents your personality.

39. A bat and ball cost $1.10 IN TOTAL; The bat costs $1 more than the ball; How much does the ball cost?

40. If you could choose one superhero Utilization Review Nurse power, what would it be and why?

41. What are the decimal equivalents of 5/16 and 7/16?

42. Design an evacuation plan for where we are right now.

43. How many boxes of breakfast cereal are sold in the US every year?

44. Why are manhole covers round?

45. Move these three chairs from one end of the room to the other.

46. If you could get rid of any one of the US states, which one would you get rid of and why?

47. How many people flew out of Cork last year?

48. How would you euthanize a giraffe?

49. A shop owner can fit 8 large boxes or 10 medium boxes into a container for delivery. In one consignment,

he distributes a total of 96 boxes. If there are more large boxes than medium boxes, how many cartons did he ship?

50. How would you weigh a Boeing 747 without using scales?

51. How would you fight a bear?

52. How many barbers are there in Chicago?

53. I roll two fair dice, what is the probability that the sum is 9?

54. How do you know if anything your Utilization Review Nurse brain is comprehending is real - could it all just be in your Utilization Review Nurse brain?

55. With your Utilization Review Nurse eyes closed, tell me step-by-step how to tie my shoes.

56. What is the angle between the hour-hand and minute-hand of a clock at [time]?

57. How many trees are there in NYC's Central Park?

58. Please take this pen and sell it to me. Tell me about its design, Utilization Review Nurse features, benefits and values.

59. How many golf balls can fit in a school bus?

Listening

1. How can you determine how well you listen?

2. Do you ask eliciting Utilization Review Nurse questions such as What do you mean?

3. Do you think there is a Utilization Review Nurse difference between hearing and listening?

4. When is listening important in your Utilization Review Nurse job?

5. Give an Utilization Review Nurse example of a time when you made a mistake because you did not listen well to what someone had to say

6. What do you do to show people that you are listing to them?

7. When is listening important on your Utilization Review Nurse job? When is listening difficult?

8. How can you empower and motivate the Utilization Review Nurse team?

9. How do you know when someone is listening to you?

10. When you are a listener, how can you encourage a speaker?

11. How can you know the gestures you use are effective?

12. Can you make a simple Utilization Review Nurse story based on a picture?

13. Are you listening, involving and encouraging?

14. When you face a Utilization Review Nurse problem, what do you do?

15. What did you want to do when you graduated?

16. Do you have good vocabulary Utilization Review Nurse skills?

17. How do you give Utilization Review Nurse staff motivating feedback?

18. Please give me an Utilization Review Nurse example of a time when youve demonstrated good listening skills?

19. How often do you have to rely on Utilization Review Nurse information you have gathered from others when talking to them? What kinds of problems have you had? What happened?

20. What do you do when you think someone is not listening to you?

21. Are you good at listening?

22. When is listening important on your Utilization Review Nurse job?

23. How do you acquire a second language?

24. What Utilization Review Nurse challenges have you faced while listening?

25. What do you do to show people that you are listening to them?

Organizational

1. What do you do when your schedule is suddenly interrupted? Give an Utilization Review Nurse example

2. Give me an Utilization Review Nurse example of a project that best describes your organizational skills

3. Describe a time when you had to make a difficult choice between your personal and professional Utilization Review Nurse life

4. How do you decide what gets top priority when scheduling your time?

Problem Resolution

1. Give an Utilization Review Nurse example of when you 'went to the source' to address a conflict. Do you feel trust levels were improved as a result?

2. There is more than one Utilization Review Nurse way to solve a problem. Give an example from your recent work experience that would illustrate this

3. Give a specific Utilization Review Nurse example of a time when you used good judgment and logic in solving a problem

4. Give an Utilization Review Nurse example of a problem which you faced on any job that you have had and tell how you went about solving it

5. Tell us about a Utilization Review Nurse situation in which you had to separate the person from the issue when working to resolve issues

6. Tell us about a recent Utilization Review Nurse success you had with an especially difficult employee/co-worker

7. Tell us about a time when you identified a potential Utilization Review Nurse problem and resolved the situation before it became serious

8. Describe a time in which you were faced with Utilization Review Nurse problems or stresses which tested your coping skills. What did you do?

9. Some Utilization Review Nurse problems require developing a unique approach. Tell about a time when

you were able to develop a different problem-solving approach

10. Sometimes we need to remain calm on the outside when we are really upset on the inside. Give an Utilization Review Nurse example of a time that this happened to you

11. Describe a time when you facilitated a creative Utilization Review Nurse solution to a problem between two employees

12. Describe a Utilization Review Nurse situation where you had a conflict with another individual, and how you dealt with it. What was the outcome? How do you feel about it?

13. Sometimes the only Utilization Review Nurse way to resolve a defense or conflict is through negotiation and compromise. Tell about a time when you were able to resolve a difficult situation by finding some common ground

14. Utilization Review Nurse Problems occur in almost all work relationships. Describe a time when you had to cope with the resentment or hostility of a subordinate or co-worker

Introducing Change

1. What media are you using for Utilization Review Nurse communication, and what is most effective?

2. What specific Utilization Review Nurse actions are your managers taking to support you / your project?

3. When is the last time you had to introduce a new Utilization Review Nurse idea or procedure to people on this job? How did you do it?

4. Have you ever had to introduce a Utilization Review Nurse policy change to your work group? How did you do it?

5. Do you know what your Utilization Review Nurse role could be in implementing a performance management system?

6. What training did you receive?

7. How have you articulated the reason for the change?

8. How do you propose to measure Utilization Review Nurse performance or the achievement of any projects objectives?

9. Do people in your current work encourage each other to support the change initiatives within the organisation?

10. Have you ever met Utilization Review Nurse

resistance when implementing a new idea or policy to a work group? How did you deal with it? What happened?

11. What will you do to ensure that you will be able to transfer the Utilization Review Nurse knowledge and skills obtained from your previous experiences to other colleagues?

12. How well managed did you think a major change was?

13. What support are you getting from your Utilization Review Nurse management team, sponsor etc?

14. How would you define the Utilization Review Nurse culture (the way you do things around here) within your current work environment?

15. Were you able to do your Utilization Review Nurse job as well as before after a major change?

16. Are you familiar with the content of a Utilization Review Nurse performance management system?

17. What disruption did you feel?

18. Do you understand the purpose of implementing a Utilization Review Nurse performance management system?

19. What Utilization Review Nurse qualities do you possess that will lead us to nominate your over other candidates?

Ambition

1. Are there educational opportunities you need on the Utilization Review Nurse job?

2. Is ambition inherently sinful?

3. What would be the Utilization Review Nurse success criteria for us in the coming years?

4. How many Utilization Review Nurse hours a day do you put into your work? What were your study patterns at school?

5. What Utilization Review Nurse sorts of things have you done to become better qualified for your career?

6. What supports do you need in getting and keeping a Utilization Review Nurse job?

7. When you disagree with your Utilization Review Nurse manager, what do you do? Give an example

8. What Utilization Review Nurse kinds of jobs interest you?

9. What are your favorite Utilization Review Nurse things, Utilization Review Nurse things to do and places to go?

10. Who buys our Utilization Review Nurse product and services and why?

11. What Utilization Review Nurse projects have you

started on your own recently? What prompted you to get started?

12. Are there any barriers to your employment?

13. What are you good at, proud of?

14. How collectively can we make a measurable Utilization Review Nurse difference?

15. What would your best Utilization Review Nurse day/worst Utilization Review Nurse day, look like?

16. Tell us about the last time that you undertook a project that Utilization Review Nurse demanded a lot of initiative

17. What frustrates or bores you?

18. What do others say about you?

19. Which Utilization Review Nurse strategy are you most interested in discussing?

20. Give two Utilization Review Nurse examples of things you've done in previous jobs that demonstrate your willingness to work hard

21. Give an Utilization Review Nurse example of an important goal that you set in the past. Tell about your success in reaching it

22. What is the most competitive work Utilization Review Nurse situation you have experienced? How did you handle it? What was the result?

23. If you are working now, How is your Utilization Review Nurse job?

24. What did you learn from where you've been, past experience?

25. What Utilization Review Nurse jobs have you had in the past?

26. Utilization Review Nurse Ideas for action: how can we press fast forward in our markets?

27. What are the Utilization Review Nurse key market and consumer trends relevant to our industry?

28. What Utilization Review Nurse relationships, if any, exist between your self-confidence and ambition?

29. Utilization Review Nurse Ideas for action: how can we press fast forward in innovation?

30. If you aren t working, what are you doing?

31. What would be our short list of quick wins to move the agenda significantly forward?

32. When you have a lot of work to do, how do you get it all done? Give an Utilization Review Nurse example?

33. Would you relocate for a good Utilization Review Nurse job?

34. Are you looking for opportunity for growth and

advancement on the Utilization Review Nurse job?

35. Tell us about a time when you had to go above and beyond the call of duty in order to get a Utilization Review Nurse job done

36. What was the best Utilization Review Nurse idea that you came up with in your career? How did you apply it?

37. How will you measure Utilization Review Nurse success?

38. What is the riskiest Utilization Review Nurse decision you have made? What was the situation? What happened?

39. Tell us about a time when a Utilization Review Nurse job had to be completed and you were able to focus your attention and efforts to get it done

40. Tell us about a time when you were particularly effective on prioritizing Utilization Review Nurse tasks and completing a project on schedule

41. There are times when we work without close Utilization Review Nurse supervision or support to get the job done. Tell us about a time when you found yourself in such a situation and how things turned out

42. Is there anything else I need to learn to move forward?

43. In the Utilization Review Nurse future, how would

you prefer to divide your time in any area?

44. What Utilization Review Nurse kinds of challenges did you face on your last job? Give an example of how you handled them

45. How much of your time do you spend doing what you want to do?

46. Describe a time when you made a Utilization Review Nurse suggestion to improve the work in your organization

47. How can we press fast forward with our people and Utilization Review Nurse skills?

48. How can we deploy existing Utilization Review Nurse knowledge and new, innovative solutions and technologies and make them more readily available to those who need them?

49. What impact did you have in your last Utilization Review Nurse job?

50. Tell us how you keep your Utilization Review Nurse job knowledge current with the on going changes in the industry

51. What is your sense of how equal men and women are in your field?

52. Why are science, Utilization Review Nurse technology and innovation essential for the achievement of our Goals?

53. Which Utilization Review Nurse key barriers to

growth can you help to reduce or remove?

54. What could you do to impact the metrics that are most relevant to us?

55. What do we mean by innovation?

56. Describe a project or Utilization Review Nurse idea that was implemented primarily because of your efforts. What was your role? What was the outcome?

Scheduling

1. How did you go about making Utilization Review Nurse job assignments?

2. How did you assign priorities to Utilization Review Nurse jobs?

3. Describe the most difficult scheduling Utilization Review Nurse problem you have faced

4. When all have been over-loaded, how do your people meet Utilization Review Nurse job assignments?

Self Assessment

1. Describe a Utilization Review Nurse situation in which you were able to use persuasion to successfully convince someone to see things your way

2. If there were one Utilization Review Nurse area you've always wanted to improve upon, what would that be?

3. What do you consider to be your professional Utilization Review Nurse strengths? Give me a specific example using this attribute in the workplace

4. What Utilization Review Nurse goal have you set for yourself that you have successfully achieved?

5. Tell us about a time when you had to go above and beyond the call of duty in order to get a Utilization Review Nurse job done

6. Can you recall a time when you were less than pleased with your Utilization Review Nurse performance?

7. In what Utilization Review Nurse ways are you trying to improve yourself?

8. Give me a specific occasion in which you conformed to a Utilization Review Nurse policy with which you did not agree

9. What was the most useful criticism you ever received?

10. Give me an Utilization Review Nurse example of an

important goal that you h ad set in the past and tell me
about your success in reaching it

Career Development

1. Whats the best Utilization Review Nurse movie youve seen in the last year?

2. What specific Utilization Review Nurse steps did you take and what was your particular contribution?

3. Whos your Utilization Review Nurse mentor?

4. If you were interviewing someone for this position, what traits would you look for?

5. Who was your favorite Utilization Review Nurse manager and why?

6. What do you think of your previous Utilization Review Nurse boss?

7. Can you describe a time when your work was criticized?

8. What are your Utilization Review Nurse skills?

9. If I were to ask your last supervisor to provide you additional training or Utilization Review Nurse exposure, what would she suggest?

10. What does your appearance say about you?

11. Did you think about what the Utilization Review Nurse outcome should be?

12. What Utilization Review Nurse kind of goals would you have in mind if you got this job?

13. What would you do if you won the lottery?

14. Whats the last Utilization Review Nurse book you read?

15. Why was there a Utilization Review Nurse gap in your employment between insert date and insert date?

16. Who do you serve?

17. What are three positive Utilization Review Nurse things your last boss would say about you?

18. What do your reports reflect?

19. How would you feel about a Utilization Review Nurse job that required you to move on a regular basis?

20. What do you do in your spare time?

21. What were your Utilization Review Nurse bosses strengths/weaknesses?

22. How much do outside influences play a Utilization Review Nurse role in your job performance?

23. How do you feel about taking no for an answer?

24. Whats the most important thing you learned in school?

25. Do you think a Utilization Review Nurse leader should be feared or liked?

26. Who has impacted you most in your Utilization Review Nurse career and how?

27. What is your greatest achievement outside of work?

28. Why should I hire you?

29. Who reviews your Utilization Review Nurse data?

30. Have you ever had a conflict with a Utilization Review Nurse boss or professor?

31. What are your interests?

32. What are you looking for in Utilization Review Nurse terms of career development?

33. How long will it take you to make a Utilization Review Nurse contribution?

34. What were the responsibilities of your last position?

35. What three Utilization Review Nurse character traits would your friends use to describe you?

36. What do you know about this Utilization Review Nurse industry?

37. What else besides your schooling and experience

qualify you for this Utilization Review Nurse job?

38. What are your interest?

39. Whats your ideal Utilization Review Nurse company?

40. What do you see yourself doing 5 or 10 Utilization Review Nurse years from now?

41. How would you feel about working for someone who knows less than you?

42. Whats the most difficult Utilization Review Nurse decision youve made in the last two years and how did you come to that Utilization Review Nurse decision?

43. How do you think I rate as an interviewer?

44. What are three positive Utilization Review Nurse character traits you dont have?

45. What would be your ideal working Utilization Review Nurse situation?

46. What Utilization Review Nurse types of careers fit your skills and interest?

47. What is your greatest fear?

48. What do you look for in Utilization Review Nurse terms of culture -structured or entrepreneurial?

49. Worried Youre In A Dead-End Utilization Review

Nurse Job?

50. What do you like to do?

51. What Utilization Review Nurse education is required for your chosen career?

52. What would you think about a Utilization Review Nurse career that required a great deal of travel?

53. If you found out your Utilization Review Nurse company was doing something against the law, like fraud, what would you do?

54. What Utilization Review Nurse qualities do you feel a successful manager should have?

55. What is your Utilization Review Nurse Career Goal?

56. Utilization Review Nurse Education and/or training after high school: What colleges or training programs did you attend to prepare for your preferred occupations?

57. How would you define a positive work Utilization Review Nurse environment?

58. What was the most difficult Utilization Review Nurse period in your life, and how did you deal with it?

59. What is your greatest Utilization Review Nurse failure, and what did you learn from it?

60. What is your biggest regret and why?

61. What do you like to do for Utilization Review Nurse fun?

62. What do you ultimately want to become?

63. Related occupation: Are there other Utilization Review Nurse career fields/occupations that look like a good match for you?

64. What are some aspects of your present Utilization Review Nurse job that you enjoy/dislike?

65. What is your greatest Utilization Review Nurse weakness?

66. What Utilization Review Nurse kind of goals would you have in mind if you got this job?

67. What are your lifelong Utilization Review Nurse dreams?

68. What do you want to be?

69. What negative thing would your last Utilization Review Nurse boss say about you?

70. Have you ever been on a Utilization Review Nurse team where someone was not pulling their weight?

71. If you could choose one superhero Utilization Review Nurse power, what would it be and why?

72. Theres no right or wrong answer, but if you could be

anywhere in the Utilization Review Nurse world right now, where would you be?

73. What Utilization Review Nurse kind of car do you drive?

74. How do you handle working with people who annoy you?

75. Why did you choose your major?

76. What magazines do you subscribe to?

77. What would be your ideal working Utilization Review Nurse environment?

78. What irritates you about other people, and how do you deal with it?

79. How do you prepare for the Utilization Review Nurse career?

80. What will you miss about your present/last Utilization Review Nurse job?

81. What assignment was too difficult for you, and how did you resolve the Utilization Review Nurse issue?

82. Whats your availability?

83. How have you gone above and beyond the call of duty?

84. What Utilization Review Nurse techniques and tools do you use to keep yourself organized?

85. What was the last project you led, and what was its Utilization Review Nurse outcome?

86. What is your favorite Utilization Review Nurse memory from childhood?

87. What are you looking for in Utilization Review Nurse terms of career development?

88. What was the last project you headed up, and what was its Utilization Review Nurse outcome?

89. How would you describe your work Utilization Review Nurse style?

90. If you had to choose one, would you consider yourself a big-Utilization Review Nurse picture person or a detail-oriented person?

91. Who are your collaborators?

92. How would you define a positive work Utilization Review Nurse environment?

93. What Utilization Review Nurse questions havent I asked you?

94. How do you want to improve yourself in the next year?

95. What is your personal Utilization Review Nurse mission statement?

96. In thinking about your Utilization Review Nurse future, you must consider whats important to you in

your daily life. What would you think about a career that required a great deal of travel?

97. Why did you apply to this position?

98. What is your plan for competency attainment?

99. Have you ever been on a Utilization Review Nurse team where someone was not pulling their own weight?

100. Identify what is unique or special about you. How have you gone above and beyond the call of duty?

101. Are you a Utilization Review Nurse team player?

102. Give me an Utilization Review Nurse example of a time you did something wrong. How did you handle it?

103. How can YOU monitor your Utilization Review Nurse data?

104. Was there a person in your Utilization Review Nurse career who really made a difference?

105. What Utilization Review Nurse kind of personality do you work best with and why?

106. What do you look for in Utilization Review Nurse terms of culture -- structured or entrepreneurial?

Selecting and Developing People

1. Tell me about a time when you did something completely different from the plan and/or assignment. Why?

2. How many Utilization Review Nurse hours a day do you put into your work?

3. What Utilization Review Nurse company plans have you developed?

4. What is the most competitive Utilization Review Nurse situation you have experienced?

5. What Utilization Review Nurse kind of decisions do you make rapidly?

6. What Utilization Review Nurse kind of thought process did you go through before meeting us here today?

7. Have you ever participated in a Utilization Review Nurse task group?

8. How have you used a question to probe for more Utilization Review Nurse information when a person is being evasive?

9. Give me an Utilization Review Nurse example of a time you had to adjust quickly to changes over which you had no control. What was the impact of the change on you?

10. How do you typically stay in the Utilization Review Nurse information loop and monitor your staffs

performance?

11. How did you ensure that another person understood?

12. Have you ever had to introduce a Utilization Review Nurse policy change to your work group?

13. How do you assemble Utilization Review Nurse information?

14. What Utilization Review Nurse kinds of challenges did you face on your last job?

15. Looking back when your Utilization Review Nurse career started to gel, what were your goals?

16. How did you go about identifying the issues?

17. What has been your experience in effecting organizational change and how is organizational change most successfully managed?

18. Describe a Utilization Review Nurse situation that required you to do a number of things at the same time. How did you handle it?

19. Do you regret any Utilization Review Nurse decision?

20. What was your biggest Utilization Review Nurse success in hiring someone? What did you do?

21. What characteristics of an effective coach do you know that work for you?

22. How did you feel you showed respect for another person?

23. Which of your Utilization Review Nurse jobs had the most rapid change?

24. Tell us about a time that you had to work on a Utilization Review Nurse team that did not get along. What happened?

25. When was the last time that you thought outside of the box and how did you do it?

26. What was your biggest mistake in hiring someone? What happened? How did you deal with the Utilization Review Nurse situation?

27. What have you done to develop your subordinates? Give an Utilization Review Nurse example

28. Tell us about the most difficult challenge you faced in trying to work co-operatively with someone who did not share the same Utilization Review Nurse ideas?

29. How do you manage and maintain your composure?

30. How do you show a person that you have understood what they have said?

31. What strategies would you utilize to maintain confidentiality when pressured by others?

32. Gaining the cooperation of others can be difficult.

Give a specific Utilization Review Nurse example of when you had to do that, and what challenges you faced. What was the outcome?

33. How do you get subordinates to work at their Utilization Review Nurse peak potential?

34. When you have Utilization Review Nurse difficulty persuading someone to your point of view, what do you do?

35. Describe a project or Utilization Review Nurse idea that was implemented primarily because of your efforts. What was your role?

36. What has been your Utilization Review Nurse contribution to strengthen the long-term stability of your business unit?

37. How did you react when faced with constant time Utilization Review Nurse pressure?

38. Do you often ask yourself; 'What are the high-performing policies, processes and practices that will help generate my deliverables required to support my companys Utilization Review Nurse strategy?'

39. Give me an Utilization Review Nurse example of a time on the job when you disagreed with your boss or a higher-level manager. What were your options for settling the conflict?

40. What, in your Utilization Review Nurse opinion, are the key ingredients in guiding and maintaining successful relationships?

41. What administrative paperwork do you have?

42. Please describe a time when you were less than pleased with your Utilization Review Nurse performance. How did you address this?

43. When was the last time you made a Utilization Review Nurse key decision on the spur of the moment?

44. How would you estimate the cost of providing a new training Utilization Review Nurse program for mid-level managers?

45. Tell me about a time you were faced with conflicting priorities. How did you resolve the conflict?

46. Have you ever been in a position where you had to lead a Utilization Review Nurse group of peers?

47. Please tell us the number and Utilization Review Nurse types of staff you have supervised and what differences, if any would you foresee in managing administrative vs. technical staff?

48. What have you done to further your own professional Utilization Review Nurse development in the past 5 years?

49. What have you done to support Utilization Review Nurse diversity at your previous employers?

50. Tell us about a recent successful experience in making a Utilization Review Nurse speech or presentation. How

did you prepare?

51. What have you done to influence an Utilization Review Nurse outcome?

52. What do you consider to be your professional Utilization Review Nurse strengths?

53. What is your vision for our Quality Improvement Utilization Review Nurse culture?

54. Describe the project or Utilization Review Nurse situation that best demonstrates your analytical abilities. What was your role?

55. What Utilization Review Nurse kinds of oral presentations have you made?

56. Have you ever been caught unaware by a Utilization Review Nurse problem or obstacle that you had not foreseen?

57. What Utilization Review Nurse kinds of data and technical information do you review?

58. Tell us about the most effective Utilization Review Nurse presentation you have made. What was the topic?

59. How do you verify that you understand what someone has told you?

60. Can you tell about a time when you chose to trust someone?

61. How would you provide Utilization Review Nurse

feedback to me?

62. Do you have a strategic plan?

63. Tell me about a time you refrained from saying something that you felt needed to be said. Do you regret your Utilization Review Nurse decision?

64. Have you had to sell an Utilization Review Nurse idea to your co-workers, classmates or group?

65. When you have a new Utilization Review Nurse problem situation, how do you go about making a decision?

66. Describe a major change that occurred in a Utilization Review Nurse job that you held. What did you do to adapt to this change?

67. What, if anything, did you do to mitigate negative consequences of your Utilization Review Nurse decisions to people?

68. How do you evaluate the productivity / effectiveness of your subordinates?

69. Have you ever been caught unaware by a Utilization Review Nurse problem or obstacles that you had not foreseen?

70. Has a Utilization Review Nurse problem or obstacles that you had not foreseen ever caught you unaware?

71. How do you assign priorities to Utilization Review Nurse jobs?

72. Describe a Utilization Review Nurse situation where you, at first, resisted a change at work and later accepted it. What, specifically, changed your mind?

73. What Utilization Review Nurse kinds of things really get you excited?

74. Why were you promoted in your last Utilization Review Nurse job?

75. Give me an Utilization Review Nurse example of when someone brought you a new idea that was unique or unusual. What did you do?

76. Give me an Utilization Review Nurse example of a time you worked particularly well under a great deal of pressure. How did you handle the situation?

77. What new or unusual Utilization Review Nurse ideas have you developed on your job?

78. Can you give us an Utilization Review Nurse example of a difficult interaction or conflict you have had with a supervisor or subordinate and how you might handle a similar situation differently (or the same) in the future?

79. How do you determine priorities in scheduling your time?

80. Have you ever been overloaded with work?

81. What one or two Utilization Review Nurse things from your prior experience and/or education do you see as being the most relevant and valuable to succeed in

this position?

82. What was the biggest mistake you have had when delegating work?

83. Have you ever been a project Utilization Review Nurse leader?

84. What approach do you take in communicating with people?

85. Tell me about a time you came up with a new Utilization Review Nurse idea. Were you able to get it approved?

86. Have you ever had a subordinate whose Utilization Review Nurse performance was consistently marginal?

87. What Utilization Review Nurse performance standards do you have for your unit?

88. When is the last time you had to introduce a new Utilization Review Nurse idea or procedure to people on the job?

89. Tell me about a disagreement that you found difficult to handle. Why was it difficult?

90. What could you have done to be more effective?

91. What were your annual Utilization Review Nurse goals at you most current employer?

92. Tell me about your typical Utilization Review Nurse

day. How much time do you spend on the phone?

93. How do you involve people in developing your units Utilization Review Nurse goals?

94. What do you do if someone at work tries to Utilization Review Nurse pressure you to do something?

95. How would you prioritize competing responsibilities, if they came in conflict?

96. What was your biggest mistake in hiring someone?

97. Is your personal Utilization Review Nurse mission statement clear, concise, and describes what you intend to accomplish?

98. How much time do you spend on the phone?

99. Tell me about a time when you had to help two peers settle a Utilization Review Nurse dispute. How did you go about identifying the issues?

100. Please give your best Utilization Review Nurse example of working cooperatively as a team member to accomplish an important goal. What was the goal or objective?

101. Describe the Utilization Review Nurse types of teams you have been involved with. What were your roles?

102. Have you ever done a research paper?

103. What specific Utilization Review Nurse actions do you take to improve relationships?

104. How do you go about establishing rapport with a Utilization Review Nurse customer?

105. What Utilization Review Nurse sorts of things did you do at school/work that was beyond expectations?

106. Tell us about a time when you did something completely different from the plan and/or assignment. Why?

107. How do you learn about a Utilization Review Nurse product or a process?

108. When have you had to produce Utilization Review Nurse results without sufficient guidelines?

109. Tell me about Utilization Review Nurse setbacks you have faced. How did you deal with them?

110. What were your roles?

111. When you have a lot of work to do, how do you get it all done?

112. Tell us about a recent Utilization Review Nurse job or experience that you would describe as a real learning experience?

113. What do you do when youre having Utilization Review Nurse trouble solving a problem?

114. Have you ever worked in a Utilization Review Nurse situation where the rules and guidelines were not clear?

115. How do you ensure your Utilization Review Nurse staff is clear about which issues warrant your attention, the information you need, and delineation of authority?

116. What have you done to improve the short-Utilization Review Nurse term strength of your business unit?

117. What Utilization Review Nurse role have you typically played as a member of a team?

118. When was the last time you were in a crisis?

119. How do you communicate Utilization Review Nurse goals to subordinates?

120. How do you coach an employee in completing a new assignment?

121. Have you ever met Utilization Review Nurse resistance when implementing a new idea or policy to a work group?

122. What Utilization Review Nurse kind of mentoring and training style do you have?

123. How do you handle Utilization Review Nurse problems with customers?

124. How do you go about developing Utilization Review Nurse information to make a decision?

125. What Utilization Review Nurse projects have you started on your own recently?

126. Describe the worst on-the-Utilization Review Nurse job crisis you had to solve. How did you manage and maintain your composure?

127. What Utilization Review Nurse kinds of problems have you had coordinating technical projects?

128. What strategies do you use when faced with more Utilization Review Nurse tasks than time to do them?

129. What have you done to develop the professional Utilization Review Nurse skills of your direct reports?

130. Have you ever been a Utilization Review Nurse member of a group where two of the Utilization Review Nurse members did not work well together?

131. Describe how your position contributes to our Utilization Review Nurse goals. What are our Utilization Review Nurse goals?

132. What Utilization Review Nurse kinds of communication situations cause you difficulty?

133. What do you like about being in charge?

134. How do you make sure you have the Utilization Review Nurse skills to implement the changes that will

come your way and become a strategic asset?

135. What has been your approach for bringing individuals on board who may be resistant to change?

136. How did you go about making changes (step by step)?

137. Describe the most challenging negotiation in which you were involved. What did you do?

138. How quickly do you make Utilization Review Nurse decisions?

139. Have you ever been in a Utilization Review Nurse situation where you had to bargain with someone?

140. How do you go about setting Utilization Review Nurse goals with employees?

141. When is the last time you had a disagreement with a peer?

142. What Utilization Review Nurse kinds of writing have you done?

143. When you disagree with your Utilization Review Nurse manager, what do you do?

144. How many Utilization Review Nurse projects do you work on at once?

145. What did you not like about being in charge?

146. What do you do when priorities change quickly?

147. What are your go-to options for settling a conflict?

148. How Do You Motivate Utilization Review Nurse Employees?

149. Describe a time when you felt that a Utilization Review Nurse planned change was inappropriate. What did you do?

150. How do you change an existing Utilization Review Nurse culture to one where it is a Quality Improvement Utilization Review Nurse culture?

151. What Utilization Review Nurse kinds of problems have you had?

152. How would you define a good working atmosphere?

153. How have your Utilization Review Nurse sales skills improved over the past three years?

154. How often do you discuss a subordinates Utilization Review Nurse performance with him/her?

155. What was the most stressful Utilization Review Nurse situation you have faced?

156. Describe a time where you were faced with Utilization Review Nurse problems or stressful situations that tested your coping skills. What did you do?

157. What sort of work Utilization Review Nurse hours do you normally put in?

158. Have you ever had Utilization Review Nurse difficulty getting others to accept your ideas?

159. How did you prepare?

160. What about this particular position and/or Utilization Review Nurse organization most interests you?

161. Give an Utilization Review Nurse example of when you went to the source to address a conflict. Do you feel trust levels were improved as a result?

162. Have you ever worked with a Utilization Review Nurse colleague to solve a problem?

163. When do you give positive Utilization Review Nurse feedback to people?

164. What was your biggest Utilization Review Nurse success in hiring someone?

165. When is the last time you had to introduce a new Utilization Review Nurse idea or procedure to people on this job?

166. How do you typically confront subordinates when Utilization Review Nurse results are unacceptable?

167. Give me an Utilization Review Nurse example of

when you were responsible for an error or mistake. What was the outcome?

168. If there were one Utilization Review Nurse area youve always wanted to improve upon, what would that be?

169. Your supervisor left you an assignment, then left for a week. You cant reach him/her and you cant do the assignment. What would you do?

170. Do you feel trust levels were improved as a result of your Utilization Review Nurse actions in a certain situation?

171. Describe how you develop a project Utilization Review Nurse teams goals and project plan?

172. How do you go about establishing rapport with a parent or community Utilization Review Nurse member?

173. Tell me about a time when you demonstrated too much initiative?

174. Tell us about a work experience where you had to work closely with others. How did it go?

175. What innovative Utilization Review Nurse procedures have you developed?

176. Have you ever dealt with a Utilization Review Nurse situation where communications were poor?

177. Tell me about a time you felt your Utilization

Review Nurse team was under too much pressure. What did you do about it?

178. How do you go about setting Utilization Review Nurse goals with subordinates?

179. What Utilization Review Nurse kinds of decisions are most difficult for you?

180. What specific Utilization Review Nurse things have you done to improve relations with parents?

181. What do you do when you are faced with an obstacle to an important project?

182. How do you adapt to change?

183. What do you do when your time schedule or project plan is upset by unforeseen circumstances?

184. What measures have you taken to make someone from a minority Utilization Review Nurse group feel comfortable in an environment that was obviously uncomfortable with his or her presence?

185. How do you resolve conflict?

186. What makes your Utilization Review Nurse communication effective?

187. Describe the most difficult working Utilization Review Nurse relationship you have had with an individual. What specific actions did you take to improve the Utilization Review Nurse relationship?

188. Tell me about a Utilization Review Nurse situation when it was important for you to pay attention to details. How did you handle it?

189. How do you go about making cold calls?

190. What did you learn from your current Utilization Review Nurse job or experience?

191. Tell me how you go about delegating work?

192. What was your Utilization Review Nurse role?

193. What were your annual Utilization Review Nurse goals at your most current employer?

194. What do you do when your schedule is suddenly interrupted?

195. What was the best Utilization Review Nurse idea that you came up with in your career?

196. How do you organize and plan for major Utilization Review Nurse projects?

197. How do you handle Utilization Review Nurse problems with colleagues?

198. What were the change/transition Utilization Review Nurse skills that you used?

199. Have you ever had to settle conflict between two people on the Utilization Review Nurse job?

200. Tell me about your impact on Utilization Review Nurse sales/revenue/cost savings over the past three years. What have you done to influence it?

201. What new Utilization Review Nurse business opportunities did you recognize while at you last employer?

202. How do you typically deal with conflict?

203. What were your long-Utilization Review Nurse range plans at you most recent employer?

204. What is the most competitive work Utilization Review Nurse situation you have experienced?

205. What have you done to develop your subordinates?

206. Give me an Utilization Review Nurse example of a time you had to think quickly on your feet to extricate yourself from a difficult situation?

207. What was your most difficult Utilization Review Nurse decision in the last 6 months?

208. How would you describe the amount of structure, Utilization Review Nurse direction, and feedback that you need to excel?

209. Do you naturally Utilization Review Nurse delegate responsibilities, or do you expect your direct reports to come to you for added responsibilities?

210. Tell us about a time that you successfully adapted to a culturally different Utilization Review Nurse

environment. What skills made you successful?

211. How do you present your position?

212. Have you ever had to make a major Utilization Review Nurse decision on your own?

213. How have you helped cross-functional groups work together?

214. What Utilization Review Nurse goals have you met?

215. What have you done to make sure that your subordinates can be productive?

216. What do you do when someone opposes your point of view?

217. What Utilization Review Nurse skills made you successful?

218. What do you do when you have multiple priorities?

219. Have you ever had a Utilization Review Nurse situation where you had a number of alternatives to choose from?

220. What have you done to further your Utilization Review Nurse knowledge/understanding about diversity?

221. How do you get subordinates to produce at a high level?

222. Tell me about a time when you had to sacrifice quality to meet a deadline. How did you handle it?

223. In Utilization Review Nurse terms of managing your staff do you expect more than you inspect or vice versa?

224. What could you have done to be more effective at a previous Utilization Review Nurse job?

225. Have you ever had to sell an Utilization Review Nurse idea to your co-workers or group?

226. What have you done to get ahead?

227. What has been your major work related disappointment?

228. How do you handle Utilization Review Nurse performance reviews?

229. Tell me about a time when you had to resolve a Utilization Review Nurse difference of opinion with a coworker/customer/supervisor. How did you feel you showed respect for that person?

230. Describe the most difficult Utilization Review Nurse problem you had to solve. What was the situation and what did you do?

231. Tell us me about an important Utilization Review Nurse goal that you set in the past. Were you successful?

232. What is the riskiest Utilization Review Nurse

decision you have made?

233. Give me a recent Utilization Review Nurse example of a situation you have faced when the pressure was on. What happened?

234. What have you done to improve the Utilization Review Nurse skills of your subordinates?

235. What are the most challenging documents you had to create?

236. Where do you see your Utilization Review Nurse career?

237. Tell us about a Utilization Review Nurse situation when it was important for you to pay attention to details. How did you handle it?

238. Have you ever had a subordinate whose work was always marginal?

239. How well has your Utilization Review Nurse business/facility/group performed?

240. Trust requires personal accountability. Can you tell about a time when you chose to trust someone?

241. Have you ever had to persuade a peer or Utilization Review Nurse manager to accept an idea that you knew they would not like?

242. How will you determine what issues to bring to your supervisor, which to Utilization Review Nurse delegate to staff and which to resolve yourself?

243. How did you prepare for today?

244. Tell us about a Utilization Review Nurse problem that you solved in a unique or unusual way. What was the outcome?

245. What, if anything, did you do to resolve Utilization Review Nurse difficulties related to trust issues?

246. What have you done or would you do to improve a Utilization Review Nurse situation which negatively impacts results?

247. How well has your Utilization Review Nurse business unit performed?

248. How do you go about making important Utilization Review Nurse decisions?

249. What Utilization Review Nurse solution are you the proudest of?

250. What Utilization Review Nurse sorts of things did you do at school that was beyond expectations?

251. One More Time: How Do You Motivate Utilization Review Nurse Employees?

252. What Utilization Review Nurse goals did you miss?

253. How often do you have to rely on Utilization Review Nurse information you have gathered from others when talking to them?

254. Describe a time in which you were faced with Utilization Review Nurse problems or stresses that tested your coping skills. What did you do?

255. Have you ever had to persuade a Utilization Review Nurse group to accept a proposal or idea?

256. Tell me about the most effective Utilization Review Nurse presentation you have made. What was the topic?

257. How would you define Utilization Review Nurse success for someone in your chosen career?

258. Tell me about the most difficult change you have had to make in your professional Utilization Review Nurse career. How did you manage the change?

259. What was the most difficult Utilization Review Nurse decision you have had to make?

260. Tell us about the last time you had to negotiate with someone. What was the most difficult part?

261. What were your long-Utilization Review Nurse range plans at your most recent employer?

262. Do you consider yourself a macro or Utilization Review Nurse micro manager?

263. How do you disseminate Utilization Review Nurse information to other people?

Resolving Conflict

1. Have you ever been in a Utilization Review Nurse situation where you had to settle an argument between two friends (or people you knew)? What did you do? What was the result?

2. Have you ever had to settle conflict between two people on the Utilization Review Nurse job? What was the situation and what did you do?

3. Describe a time when you took personal accountability for a conflict and initiated Utilization Review Nurse contact with the individual(s) involved to explain your actions

4. Tell us about a time when you had to help two peers settle a Utilization Review Nurse dispute. How did you go about identifying the issues? What did you do? What was the result?

Negotiating

1. Is there an Utilization Review Nurse action you can take to help develop trust (provide information, demonstrate sincerity)?

2. Have you ever been in a Utilization Review Nurse situation where you had to bargain with someone? How did you feel about this? What did you do? Give an example

3. How much will you ask for?

4. Have you ever had the need to help your Utilization Review Nurse group get on the same page to manage a conflict, ready for a transaction, or make a decision?

5. What was the most difficult part?

6. Are the offers at least as good as your best Alternative to negotiated agreement?

7. Are there any Time Bombs in your proposed offers?

8. What changes were you able to accommodate and why?

9. Reservation Point: What is the least you are willing to accept?

10. Do you have any Utilization Review Nurse questions?

11. How do you say yes, no, and maybe?

12. What do you need me to feel?

13. How do you call an intermission?

14. Will the salary meet your needs?

15. How did you resolve it?

16. How did you present your position?

17. What does your Utilization Review Nurse organization / chain of command / team want to have happen?

18. What do you need to learn?

19. Sequencing – How do you want to sequentially organize your negotiation?

20. Tell us about the last time you had to negotiate with someone

21. Who can influence the Utilization Review Nurse outcome of the talks, besides the one(s) you will negotiate with?

22. Identify your stakeholders. What are the stakeholders positions and interests?

23. What should you do if you have no alternatives to agreement and the other side is big and powerful?

24. How does the salary match the research you did and your Utilization Review Nurse range?

25. Why are they talking to you?

26. From your Utilization Review Nurse perspective, what are the overarching issues?

27. Is there anything else you can do in Utilization Review Nurse terms of the offer?

28. What lessons can you extract from this negotiation to help Utilization Review Nurse mentor others?

29. Ask yourself what they other Utilization Review Nurse sides BATNA may be. Why are they talking to you?

30. What Utilization Review Nurse questions/answers about the other side might strengthen your position during negotiations and thus increase your chances of a successful outcome?

31. How do you prepare for a negotiation?

32. Do you send the Utilization Review Nurse information piecemeal, or wait to collect all the Utilization Review Nurse information and send one bill?

33. What aspect of this negotiation was most challenging for you?

34. Closure – how do you plan on converting from divergent thinking (option Utilization Review Nurse development) to convergent thinking (solution selection)?

35. What will your opening statement be the first 90 seconds?

36. What do you think they want the Utilization Review Nurse situation to be AFTER the negotiations conclude (what is/are the opposites perceptions of longterm interest(s))?

37. Describe the most challenging negotiation in which you were involved. What did you do? What were the Utilization Review Nurse results for you? What were the Utilization Review Nurse results for the other party?

38. Your BATNA?

39. Which matters most to you?

40. Will you make the first offer?

41. How did you prepare for it?

42. What is your assessment of the level of trust between you and the opposite?

43. Do the offers satisfy the Interests youve listed?

44. What if the other side plays dirty, how should you respond?

45. Where might your interests and the interests of the opposite coincide?

46. What is your walk away point?

Business Acumen

1. Have you ever been engaged in Utilization Review Nurse team sales?

2. Describe a time when you took a new Utilization Review Nurse job that required a much different set of skills from what you had. How did you go about acquiring the needed skills?

3. What experience do you have with financial planning and analysis?

4. Are you able to perform the essential functions of the Utilization Review Nurse job?

5. What Is Your Capacity for Trust?

6. How do you discuss a Utilization Review Nurse policy with your staff?

7. Are there any Utilization Review Nurse types of marketing that you consider unethical?

8. Give an Utilization Review Nurse example of a time when you had to quickly change project priorities. How did you do it?

9. What Utilization Review Nurse kinds of investigations have you had to complete?

10. What are your Utilization Review Nurse career path interests?

11. Have you ever been involved in a department or Utilization Review Nurse company reorganization or big

change?

12. We are seeking Utilization Review Nurse employees who focus on detail. What means have you used to keep from making mistakes?

13. Tell me about a time when working in a different country you had to adapt to the Utilization Review Nurse culture. What adaptations did you have to make?

14. You are a committee Utilization Review Nurse member and disagree with a point or decision. How will you respond?

15. Can you tell me about a time during your previous employment when you suggested a better Utilization Review Nurse way to perform a process?

16. What have you done to help your human Utilization Review Nurse resources department to become a strategic partner?

17. Tell me about a time when you thought someone wasnt listening to you. What did you do?

18. What employment policies have you developed or revised?

19. How would your co-workers describe your work Utilization Review Nurse style/habits?

20. In what Utilization Review Nurse ways do you consider yourself unreliable?

21. How would you define guest/client satisfaction?

22. What software have you had the most Utilization Review Nurse success supporting?

23. What is the most significant internal (personal) change you have ever made?

24. How would people you work with describe you?

25. Describe a Utilization Review Nurse situation where you have had to work in a multicultural environment and the challenges you had. How did you approach the Utilization Review Nurse situation and what was the outcome?

26. What drove you, or supported you, in making the change?

27. What type of inventory audits have you been involved in?

28. Where do you see your Utilization Review Nurse career now?

29. Describe a difficult time you have had dealing with an employee, Utilization Review Nurse customer or co-worker. Why was it difficult?

30. You have a critical Utilization Review Nurse decision to make for your department, and all alternatives will likely be unpopular with your staff. What input do you gather before deciding?

31. Do you have a personal philosophy about human

Utilization Review Nurse resources?

32. What compensation experience do you have?

33. How do you stay current with changes in employment laws, practices and other HR issues?

34. Give a specific Utilization Review Nurse example of a decision you made that was not effective. Why do you think it was not effective, and what did you do when this realization was made?

35. How can you manage this Utilization Review Nurse resistance?

36. Tell us about your Utilization Review Nurse management stylepeople, teamwork, direction?

37. So, you can work diligently on your general propensity to trust, but some people will still let you down. Does that mean you shouldnt trust?

38. What has your current Utilization Review Nurse company (or most recent employer) done in response to recent social changes?

39. How did you resolve the Utilization Review Nurse problem?

40. What is the HR structure in your current or most recent Utilization Review Nurse job?

41. Utilization Review Nurse Strategy. What was your

role?

42. Have you ever been over Utilization Review Nurse budget?

43. Was the Utilization Review Nurse success or failure of your expatriate assignments measured by your employers?

44. Describe a time when you had to deal with a difficult Utilization Review Nurse boss, co-worker or customer. How did you handle the situation?

45. What type of training/Utilization Review Nurse education did you receive in the military?

46. Tell me about your experience with IT systems?

47. Throughout your Utilization Review Nurse career have you learned more about your profession through coursework or through on the job experience?

48. Who or what drove you, or supported you, in making this Utilization Review Nurse job change?

49. Describe your most challenging encounter with month end/year end closing. How did you resolve the Utilization Review Nurse problem?

50. What was the last big project you worked on?

51. What was one of the toughest Utilization Review Nurse problems you ever solved?

52. What are the Core Utilization Review Nurse Leadership Competencies needed for your organization?

53. Have you ever faced a significant ethical Utilization Review Nurse problem at work?

54. What should your Utilization Review Nurse role be going forward?

55. Describe for me a time when you have come across questionable accounting practices. How did you handle the Utilization Review Nurse situation?

56. What do you look for when considering whether another person is trustworthy?

57. How do you go about learning how our Utilization Review Nurse organization works?

58. What was the last work-related educational Utilization Review Nurse seminar or class you attended?

59. In what Utilization Review Nurse types of situations can you answer yes and in which is the answer no?

60. How did you prepare yourself to make the change?

61. What do you do to develop Utilization Review Nurse employees you manage?

62. What did you bring to the last position you were in?

63. Can you share an Utilization Review Nurse example of a time when you developed rapport with a customer?

64. How were you rated on dependability on your last Utilization Review Nurse job?

65. What Utilization Review Nurse percentage of time did you spend on each functional area of your job?

66. When making a Utilization Review Nurse decision to terminate employment of an employee, do you find it easy because of the companys needs or difficult because of the employees needs?

67. What have you done when faced with an obstacle to an important project?

68. What do you do when someone else is late and preventing you from accomplishing your Utilization Review Nurse tasks?

69. Whats Your Financial Utilization Review Nurse Style?

70. Describe a time you recommended a change to Utilization Review Nurse procedure. What did you learn from that experience?

71. How Have You Responded to Change?

72. Could you share with us a recent Utilization Review Nurse accomplishment of which you are most proud?

73. Tell me about your Utilization Review Nurse policy development experiences. What employment policies have you developed or revised?

74. If you are hired for this position and are still with (name of Utilization Review Nurse company/ organization) five years from now, how do you think the organization will be different?

75. Whats the most valuable thing youve learned in the past year?

76. Describe the workload at your current position. How do you feel about it?

77. What Utilization Review Nurse input do you gather before deciding?

78. Tell me about a time when you had a work Utilization Review Nurse problem and didnt know what to do?

79. As our president/CEO, how would you proceed if the board of directors adopted a Utilization Review Nurse policy or program that you felt was inconsistent with the goals and mission of our company?

80. If I asked your previous/current co-workers about you, what would they say?

81. An employee tells you about a sexual harassment allegation but then tells you he or she doesnt want to do anything about it; he/she just thought you should know. How do you respond?

82. How did you go about acquiring the needed Utilization Review Nurse skills?

83. What HR metrics does your current/former Utilization Review Nurse organization monitor?

84. Describe for me a time when you have come across questionable Utilization Review Nurse business practices. How did you handle the situation?

85. Tell me about the one person who has Utilization Review Nurse influenced you the most during your career?

86. What control measures/Utilization Review Nurse techniques would you put in place to overcome risks?

87. Give me an Utilization Review Nurse example of a time when you needed to help other employees learn a new skill set. What did you do?

88. Will you be able to work this schedule?

89. Do people ever come to you for help in solving Utilization Review Nurse problems?

90. Tell me about a time when you organized, managed and motivated others on a complex Utilization Review Nurse task from beginning to end?

91. Tell me about your experience working with a board of directors. What approach and philosophy did you follow in working with boards?

92. In what situations can you say yes and in which is the answer no?

93. What experience do you have in multistate HR Utilization Review Nurse management?

94. Was there a time when you struggled to meet a deadline?

95. What would you do if faced with creating cost-cutting measures for Utilization Review Nurse benefits premiums?

96. Have you completed month end/year end closing?

97. What does servicing the sale mean to you?

98. What would be the Utilization Review Nurse steps you would take if you were responsible for reducing staff by 10 percent?

99. Describe for me a Utilization Review Nurse decision you made that would normally have been made by your supervisor?

100. A new Utilization Review Nurse policy is to be implemented organization-wide. You do not agree with this new Utilization Review Nurse policy. How do you discuss this Utilization Review Nurse policy with your staff?

101. What Utilization Review Nurse kind of experience do you have with training employees and managers?

102. Give an Utilization Review Nurse example of how you carefully considered your audience prior to communicating with them. What factors influenced your communication?

103. What year did you graduate from high school?

104. Have you ever had to persuade a peer or superior to accept an Utilization Review Nurse idea that you knew he/she would not like?

105. What aspects of the strategic-doing cycle does your Utilization Review Nurse organization/Utilization Review Nurse organization do well?

106. You're new to an Utilization Review Nurse organization. How do you go about learning how that Utilization Review Nurse organization works?

107. Under what Utilization Review Nurse kinds of conditions do you learn best?

108. What, if any, cost overrun issues did you have?

109. What vendor Utilization Review Nurse relationships were you responsible for managing?

110. Do you feel you are knowledgeable about current Utilization Review Nurse industry-related legislation or trends?

111. Have you worked under time constraints before?

112. What would you have done differently?

113. The last time that you experienced a technical Utilization Review Nurse problem during your workday, to whom did you go for help?

114. How did you start this project?

115. Do You Need To Enhance Your Utilization Review Nurse Leadership Skills?

116. What was the best training Utilization Review Nurse program in which you have participated?

117. What Utilization Review Nurse actions can you take to ensure that your interUtilization Review Nurse actions with employees and/or stakeholders are and will remain unguarded?

118. How many expatriate assignments have you completed?

119. What Utilization Review Nurse things get in the way of successful strategic doing in your organization/ organization?

120. What Utilization Review Nurse area of your last job was most challenging for you?

121. In what Utilization Review Nurse ways can you monitor comments and feedback?

122. Describe some recent Utilization Review Nurse projects you were involved in to improve accountings efficiency/effectiveness. What did you do?

123. What Utilization Review Nurse challenges might you encounter in balancing the needs of the organization and those of individuals?

124. What do you do when you know you are right and your Utilization Review Nurse boss disagrees with you?

125. If I asked several of your co-workers about your greatest strength as a Utilization Review Nurse team member, what would they tell me?

126. What brands of hardware do you feel most comfortable dealing with?

127. Tell me about a Utilization Review Nurse situation in which you lost it or did not do your best with a customer. What did you do about this?

128. Have you worked in a Utilization Review Nurse situation where an employee, vendor or supplier had a conflict of interest?

129. Can you work within the confines of a x-foot aisle?

130. Give an Utilization Review Nurse example of a time when you were trying to meet a deadline, you were interrupted, and did not make the deadline. How did you respond?

131. Have you ever been convicted of a felony?

132. What do you think is the Utilization Review Nurse role of the president/CEO in strategic planning for the organization?

133. What would your last Utilization Review Nurse boss say about how you collaborate with others?

134. What adaptations did you have to make?

135. What do you think of your last Utilization Review Nurse boss?

136. Suppose your supervisor asked you to get Utilization Review Nurse information for him or her that you knew was confidential and he/she should not have access to. What would you do?

137. How else can you, as a Utilization Review Nurse leader, build trust among your constituents, whether they are employees, those above you in rank, your peers in other organizations, the media, or the public?

138. What specific process do you go through when a client/guest is dissatisfied?

139. Does your Utilization Review Nurse organization create a culture that encourages learning and mentorship?

140. You are angry about an unfair Utilization Review Nurse decision. How do you react?

141. What strength could you leverage?

142. In what specific Utilization Review Nurse ways can you be a catalyst rather than a controller of change?

143. What characteristics do you feel are necessary for Utilization Review Nurse success as a technical support worker?

144. Do you trust others?

145. What are your Utilization Review Nurse organization s Core Values and Competencies?

146. What Utilization Review Nurse challenges did you meet along the way?

147. What Utilization Review Nurse types of behaviors do you find most annoying or frustrating in a client/customer?

148. What was the most creative thing you did in your last Utilization Review Nurse job?

149. Solutions: what specific Utilization Review Nurse actions will you take to address specific priorities?

150. What factors Utilization Review Nurse influenced your communication?

151. Have you ever given a Utilization Review Nurse presentation to a group?

152. What did you do to adjust to a change?

153. What interim systems might you need to implement?

154. What is the largest number of Utilization Review

Nurse employees you have supervised and what were their job functions?

155. Would you be willing to relocate if necessary?

156. In what Utilization Review Nurse ways or in what situations do you have the least capacity for trust?

157. What are some of the specific Utilization Review Nurse ways you demonstrate that you do what you say?

158. Whats your financial signature?

159. How did you know you needed to make the change?

160. How can you keep Utilization Review Nurse employees and/or stakeholders involved in the process?

161. What do you believe is your most honed Utilization Review Nurse skill?

162. How do you get people not under your authority to do work on your project?

163. What potential Utilization Review Nurse resistance points might you encounter?

164. Have you ever solved a Utilization Review Nurse problem that others around you could not solve?

165. Do you believe you will be remembered?

166. Have you processed payroll?

167. Does your Utilization Review Nurse organization have a formal process for career development?

168. Do You Have The Utilization Review Nurse Business Acumen For Success?

169. What Utilization Review Nurse difficulties did you experience adjusting to previous international assignments?

170. Do you have health-care coverage through your spouse?

171. Tell me about a complicated Utilization Review Nurse issue youve had to deal with. What was the Utilization Review Nurse issue?

172. Tell me about a time when you solved one Utilization Review Nurse problem but created others?

173. What support, either administrative or technical Utilization Review Nurse assistance, did you receive in your previous positions?

174. What will you gain?

175. Do you tend to assume that others can be trusted until proved otherwise, or do you wait for people to prove they are trustworthy?

176. What means have you used to keep from making

Utilization Review Nurse mistakes?

177. What mechanisms can you use to solicit employee and/or stakeholder concerns?

178. Your work Utilization Review Nurse style would complement mine?

179. Do you belong to any professional or trade organizations that are relevant to this Utilization Review Nurse job?

180. What metrics did you use to measure ongoing project status?

181. How do you analyze different options to determine which is the best alternative?

182. What clubs or social organizations do you belong to?

183. Have you ever managed a Utilization Review Nurse situation where the people or units reporting to you were in different locations?

184. In what areas would you like to develop further?

185. Have you had a non-productive Utilization Review Nurse team member on your project Utilization Review Nurse team?

186. Have you ever had to champion an unpopular change?

187. Have you had an occasion when a prior strength

actually turned out to be a Utilization Review Nurse weakness in another setting?

188. What recruiting experience do you have?

189. When you have several users experiencing computer Utilization Review Nurse problems, how do you determine which users get help first?

190. Suppose you are in a Utilization Review Nurse situation where deadlines and priorities change frequently and rapidly. How would you handle it?

191. What Utilization Review Nurse benefits experience do you have?

192. How do you determine what amount of time is reasonable for a Utilization Review Nurse task?

193. What was the most challenging employee Utilization Review Nurse performance issue youve had to deal with and how did you handle it?

194. People react differently when Utilization Review Nurse job demands are constantly changing. How do you react to this?

195. What criteria would you use to assess whether an employee is a rising star in your Utilization Review Nurse organization?

196. How many Utilization Review Nurse words per minute can you type?

197. How did you handle the Utilization Review Nurse situation?

198. What are some of the Utilization Review Nurse ways you can show respect for the knowledge, skills, and abilities of your employees or other stakeholders?

199. When was the date of your last physical exam?

200. What does Utilization Review Nurse customer mean to you?

201. What small successes can you celebrate?

202. What do you think makes a Utilization Review Nurse team of people work well together?

203. How do you think your Utilization Review Nurse clients/customers/guests would describe you and your work?

204. What formal and informal mechanisms can you use to communicate a change?

205. What is your marital status?

206. What are your major professional reading sources?

207. What are your child-care arrangements?

208. What type of Utilization Review Nurse projects have you managed in the past?

209. Have you ever worked in a virtual Utilization Review Nurse team?

210. How many Utilization Review Nurse employees do you support and in what capacity?

211. Tell me about a work nightmare you were involved in. How did you approach the Utilization Review Nurse situation and what was the outcome?

212. Describe a time when you performed a Utilization Review Nurse task outside your perceived responsibilities. What was the Utilization Review Nurse task?

213. How can you walk the talk during a change initiative?

214. How can you sustain energy and commitment to a change over time?

215. Give me an Utilization Review Nurse example of a time when you had to deal with a difficult co-worker. How did you handle the situation?

216. What is your native language?

217. Do you trust yourself?

218. Tell me about a time when big changes took place in your Utilization Review Nurse job. What did you do to adjust to the change?

219. What do you think are the best and worst parts of working in a Utilization Review Nurse team environment?

220. How would you describe your abilities as a Utilization Review Nurse business developer?

221. When it comes to giving Utilization Review Nurse information to employees that can be done either way, do you prefer to write an email/memo or talk to the employee?

222. What is more important to your profession, experience or continued Utilization Review Nurse education?

223. Have you ever worked in a union Utilization Review Nurse environment?

224. If someone asked you for Utilization Review Nurse assistance with a matter that is outside the parameters of your job description, what would you do?

225. How have you reacted when you found yourself stalled in an inefficient process?

226. In what Utilization Review Nurse ways do you consider yourself reliable?

227. Utilization Review Nurse careers grow and develop just like people do. Where do you see your Utilization Review Nurse career now?

228. In your experience, what are the essential elements of an IT disaster recovery plan?

229. When you have a lot of work to do or multiple priorities, how do you get it all done?

230. What methods do you use to make Utilization Review Nurse decisions?

231. What coaching or mentoring experience have you had?

232. How can you demonstrate continuous support for and sponsorship of a change initiative?

233. How well do you communicate with others?

234. How have you approached solving a Utilization Review Nurse problem that initially seemed insurmountable?

235. What experience have you had with tax accounting?

236. What approach and philosophy did you follow in working with boards?

237. Have you ever done a cost-benefit analysis?

238. What Utilization Review Nurse strengths did you rely on in your last position to make you successful in your work?

239. When do you think it is best to communicate in writing?

240. How would you start this project?

241. On your last expatriate assignment, what did you do to ensure that your adjustment into the new Utilization

Review Nurse environments went smoothly?

242. What is your own philosophy of Utilization Review Nurse management?

243. When theres a Utilization Review Nurse decision for a new critical process, what means do you use to communicate step-by-step processes to ensure other people understand and will complete the process correctly?

244. What languages do you read/speak/write fluently?

245. Describe a time when you lost a Utilization Review Nurse customer. What would you do differently?

246. We all have Utilization Review Nurse customers or clients. –Who are your clients and how do you identify them?

247. How do you go about deciding what Utilization Review Nurse strategy to employ when dealing with a difficult customer?

248. Describe a technical report that you had to complete. What did the report entail?

Believability

1. What were some of the most important Utilization Review Nurse things you accomplished on your last job?

2. What are your Utilization Review Nurse standards of success in your job and how do you know when you are successful?

3. What do you do differently from other (   )? Why? Give Utilization Review Nurse examples.

4. Give us an Utilization Review Nurse example of when someone brought you a new idea, particularly one that was odd or unusual. What did you do?

5. We don't always make Utilization Review Nurse decisions that everyone agrees with. Give us an example of an unpopular decision you made. How did you communicate the decision and what was the outcome?

6. Describe your ideal supervisor.

7. Describe a Utilization Review Nurse situation in which you received a new procedure or instructions with which you disagreed. What did you do?

8. Describe a Utilization Review Nurse situation in which you had to translate a broad or general directive from superiors into individual performance expectations. How did you do this and what were the results?

9. What is your Utilization Review Nurse management

style? How do you think your subordinates perceive you?

10. Utilization Review Nurse Jobs differ in the degree to which unexpected changes can disrupt daily responsibilities. Tell what you did and us about a time when this happened.

11. Give a specific Utilization Review Nurse example of how you have involved subordinates in identifying performance goals and expectations.

12. Sometimes supervisors' evaluations differ from our own. What did you do about it?

13. It is important that Utilization Review Nurse performance and other personnel issues be addressed timely. Give examples of the type of personnel issues you've confronted and how you addressed them. Including examples of the process you used for any disciplinary action taken or grievance resolved.

14. All Utilization Review Nurse jobs have their frustrations and problems. Describe some specific tasks or conditions that have been frustrating to you. Why were they frustrating and what did you do?

15. Give an Utilization Review Nurse example of how you monitor the progress your employees are making on projects or tasks you delegated.

Outgoingness

1. Tell us about a time when you delayed responding to a Utilization Review Nurse situation until you had time to review the facts, even though there was pressure to act quickly.

2. On occasion, we have to be firm and assertive in order to achieve a desired result. Tell us about a time when you had to do that.

3. How do you know if your Utilization Review Nurse customers are satisfied?

4. Describe a time when you were able to effectively communicate a difficult or unpleasant Utilization Review Nurse idea to a superior.

5. Have you ever had Utilization Review Nurse difficulty getting along with co-workers? How did you handle the situation and what was the outcome?

6. Describe some particularly trying Utilization Review Nurse customer complaints or resistance you have had to handle. How did you react? What was the outcome?

7. Tell us about a time when you had to motivate a Utilization Review Nurse group of people to get an important job done. What did you do, what was the outcome?

8. Being Utilization Review Nurse successful is hard work. Tell us about a specific achievement when you had to work especially hard to attain the Utilization Review Nurse success you desired.

9. Sooner or later we all have to deal with a Utilization Review Nurse customer who has unreasonable demands. Think of a time when you had to handle unreasonable requests. What did you do and what was the outcome?

10. Tell us about a time when you were effective in handling a Utilization Review Nurse customer complaint. Why were you effective? What was the outcome?

11. Many of us have had co-workers or managers who tested our patience. Tell us about a time when you restrained yourself to avoid conflict with a co-worker or supervisor. (restrained)

12. In Utilization Review Nurse job situations you may be pulled in many different directions at once. Tell us about a time when you had to respond to this type of situation. How did you manage yourself?

13. There are times when we need to insist on doing something a certain Utilization Review Nurse way. Give us the details surrounding a situation when you had to insist on doing something "your Utilization Review Nurse way". What was the outcome?

Unflappability

1. There are times when we all have to deal with deadlines and it can be stressful. Tell us about a time when you felt pressured at work and how you coped with it.

2. Give us an Utilization Review Nurse example of when you made a presentation to an uninterested or hostile audience. How did it turn out?

3. Give us an Utilization Review Nurse example of when you felt overly sensitive to feedback or criticism. How did you handle your feelings?

4. Tell us about a time when you put in some extra Utilization Review Nurse effort to help move a project forward. How did you do that? What happened?

5. Give us an Utilization Review Nurse example of a demanding situation when you were able to maintain your composure while others got upset.

6. Tell us about a time when you received accurate, negative Utilization Review Nurse feedback by a co-worker, boss, or customer. How did you handle the evaluation? How did it affect your work?

7. On occasion, we experience conflict with our superiors. Describe such a Utilization Review Nurse situation and tell us how you handled the conflict. What was the outcome?

8. Describe Utilization Review Nurse suggestions you have made to improve work procedures. How did it turn

out?

9. Many times, a Utilization Review Nurse job requires you to quickly shift your attention from one task to the next. Tell us about a time at work when you had to change focus onto another task. What was the outcome?

10. We have to find Utilization Review Nurse ways to tolerate and work with difficult people. Tell us about a time when you have done this.

Project Management

1. Tell us about a time when you Utilization Review Nurse influenced the outcome of a project by taking a leadership role

2. Using a specific Utilization Review Nurse example of a project, tell how you kept those involved informed of the progress

Follow-up and Control

1. How do you get Utilization Review Nurse data for performance reviews?

2. How do you keep track of what your subordinates are doing?

3. What administrative paperwork do you have? Is it useful? Why/why not?

4. How do you evaluate the productivity/effectiveness of your subordinates?

5. How did you keep track of delegated assignments?

Like-ability

1. There are times when people need extra Utilization Review Nurse assistance with difficult projects. Give us an example of when you offered Utilization Review Nurse assistance to someone with whom you worked.

2. In working with people, we find that what works with one person does not work with another. Therefore, we have to be flexible in our Utilization Review Nurse style of relating to others. Give us a specific example of when you had to vary your work Utilization Review Nurse style with a particular individual. How did it work out?

3. Give us an Utilization Review Nurse example of how you have been able to develop a close, positive relationship with one of your customers.

4. Tell us about a time when you were able to build a successful Utilization Review Nurse relationship with a difficult person.

5. Give us an Utilization Review Nurse example of how you establish an atmosphere at work where others feel comfortable in communicating their ideas, feelings and concerns.

6. Describe a particularly trying Utilization Review Nurse customer complaint or resistance you had to handle. How did you react and what was the outcome?

7. Have you ever had Utilization Review Nurse difficulty getting along with a co-worker? How did you handle the

situation and what was the outcome?

8. Tell us about a time when you needed someone's cooperation to complete a Utilization Review Nurse task and the person was uncooperative. What did you do? What was the outcome?

9. How would you describe your Utilization Review Nurse management style? How do you think your subordinates perceive you?

10. Tell us about a Utilization Review Nurse situation in which you became frustrated or impatient when dealing with a coworker. What did you do? What was the outcome?

11. It is important to remain composed at work and to maintain a positive outlook. Give us a specific Utilization Review Nurse example of when you were able to do this.

12. On occasion we may be faced with a Utilization Review Nurse situation that has escalated to become a confrontation. If you have had such an experience, tell me how you handled it. What was the outcome? Would you do anything differently today?

13. Describe a time when you weren't sure what a Utilization Review Nurse customer wanted. How did you handle the situation?

14. Many Utilization Review Nurse jobs are team-oriented where a work group is the key to success. Give us an example of a time when you worked on a team to complete a project. How did it work? What was the outcome?

15. Some people are difficult to work with. Tell us about a time when you encountered such a person. How did you handle it?

16. Having an understanding of the other person's Utilization Review Nurse perspective is crucial in dealing with customers. Give us an example of a time when you achieved success through attaining insight into the other person's Utilization Review Nurse perspective.

17. We don't always make Utilization Review Nurse decisions that everyone agrees with. Give us an example of an unpopular decision you have made. How did you communicate the decision and what was the outcome?

18. Tell us about a Utilization Review Nurse job where the atmosphere was the easiest for you to get along and function well. Describe the qualities of that work environment.

Business Systems Thinking

1. Do you agree that the more extensive a salespersons experience, the less relevant adaptability becomes to that person?

2. Are you aware of the Utilization Review Nurse relationship of sales engineeeers in new product development and customer sales?

3. To what extent are you knowledgeable of the new 6th P in the marketing mix, Poise?

4. Do you agree that a salespersons fear of change heightens ones readiness when faced with different Utilization Review Nurse performance procedures?

5. What would be the affect on our Utilization Review Nurse customers lives if you did not exist to do your work?

6. Is your current Utilization Review Nurse company properly structured for the future of market opportunities and challenges?

7. Is Six Sigma a Good Fit for our Utilization Review Nurse Business?

8. Are you aware, in general Utilization Review Nurse terms, of the functions and responsibilities of this role?

9. Do you agree that having the accessibility of creative, Utilization Review Nurse communication tools increases the possibility of creative thinking?

10. Do you agree that the higher a Utilization Review Nurse salesperson perceives the value of adaptability, the higher the likely increase in Utilization Review Nurse sales revenue?

11. Are you aware, in general Utilization Review Nurse terms, of the functions and responsibilities of marketing research firms?

12. Do you agree that the setting of the Utilization Review Nurse organization impacts how innovative its salespersons are in their selling approaches?

13. Would you agree that Offensive Marketing would be valuable for having created superior and recognized Utilization Review Nurse customer value as well as having achieved above-average profits?

14. Do you consider ethics an important aspect of doing Utilization Review Nurse business?

15. Describe how your position contributes to your organization's/unit's Utilization Review Nurse goals. What are the unit's Utilization Review Nurse goals/ mission?

16. What do you think about Utilization Review Nurse business system thinking and ethical dilemmas?

17. Whom do you serve?

18. What Do You Need From Me?

19. Do you believe our Utilization Review Nurse product

is one that will last or is the market a fad?

20. Do you agree that creativity can be taught?

21. Who Is Your Utilization Review Nurse Leadership?

22. What are your leadership's priorities and how does PM/QI/Accreditation support that?

23. Do you agree that the more authority a salespersons possesses, the higher their probability of coming up with innovative Utilization Review Nurse ideas?

24. Does our companys image match with your brands and products?

25. Who is our Utilization Review Nurse target market?

26. Do you agree that Utilization Review Nurse companies that have a more flexible atmosphere are more prone to creative thinking?

27. Are you aware of the Utilization Review Nurse relationship of sales engineers in new product development and customer sales?

28. Are you aware, in general Utilization Review Nurse terms, of the functions and responsibilities of a sales engineer?

29. To what extent are you aware of the Utilization Review Nurse company-wide applications of Poise?

30. Do you agree that Effective Marketing, through brand equity, has played an important Utilization Review Nurse role in establishing distinct advantages towards our firms marketing perceived value from its marketplace?

31. Do you feel that ones moral Utilization Review Nurse standards should equal or exceed their companys code of ethics?

32. Where, geographically, does our market have strong holds?

33. Would you feel that one of the most important assets of businesses would be its new Utilization Review Nurse product development?

34. Do you agree that creativity can be motivated through incentives?

35. Would you trust a firm whos ethical Utilization Review Nurse standards were considered to be/have been suspect?

36. To what extent do you agree that ethical Utilization Review Nurse standards begins at the highest levels of the firm?

37. Why are you really winning and losing deals?

38. What is our Utilization Review Nurse organization about and how does PM/QI/Accreditation support that?

39. Tell us about a politically complex work Utilization

Review Nurse situation in which you worked

Setting Priorities

1. Were there times that you could have used more efficiently?

2. What Utilization Review Nurse questions can you ask yourself to help you prioritize your tasks?

3. How do you determine you have a critical Utilization Review Nurse problem?

4. What Utilization Review Nurse kind of measuring stick do you use to distinguish the difference between activities that are essential versus things which are nonessential?

5. Have you ever been overloaded with work? How do you keep track of work so that it gets done on time?

6. All of us have these barriers. Name some barriers to effective time Utilization Review Nurse management in your life. Are these barriers that can be removed or avoided?

7. What strategies do you use to priorities?

8. What Utilization Review Nurse kinds of discussion do you remember about finances before or soon after your marriage?

9. Which of your Utilization Review Nurse activities was really important?

10. Do you spend too much time on some Utilization Review Nurse activities?

11. How do you schedule your time?

12. How do you manage your time?

13. Consider your energy level. Are you a morning person, or do you have more energy in the evening?

14. How do you set priorities?

15. When given an important assignment, how do you approach it?

16. Is saying no to peoples requests of you a different thing to do?

17. What are some Utilization Review Nurse steps you take to overcome procrastination?

18. How do you decided what to buy?

19. Are you a morning person, or do you have more energy in the evening?

20. How do you currently spend your time?

Index

301

highly   101
hiring   129, 150, 222-223, 230, 236
history 37, 184
hobbies   7, 142
holiday 108
holidays   106, 149
honest 22, 50, 54
honorable   60
honorably   75
hostile 280
hostility 78, 198
hour-hand   192
household   48
Humility   175
Hunger 175
identified   1, 90, 149, 197
identify 7, 10, 28, 44, 72, 76, 116, 183, 219, 248, 275
illustrate   197
imaginary   183
immature   77
immediate   47
impact 62, 96, 163, 206-207, 221, 240
impacted   47, 171, 213
impacts   244, 288
impatient   285
implement   8, 35, 115, 233, 266
important   10-11, 13, 15, 20, 24, 26, 40-41, 47, 55, 61, 65, 75,
85, 87-88, 97, 100-102, 108, 114-115, 117, 133, 135, 143, 153-154,
158, 170, 173, 180, 183, 193-194, 203, 210, 212, 218, 230, 238-239,
242-244, 258, 273, 276-278, 285, 288, 290, 292-293
impression   24
impressive   159
improve   14, 32, 39, 51, 55, 126, 147-148, 177, 206, 209,
218, 231-232, 237-238, 243-244, 263, 280
improved   197, 235-237
improving   25, 62
incentives   290
incidents   80
included   42
Including   45, 277
increase   26, 111, 121, 145, 249, 288
increases   287
increasing   32

317

practices   23, 224, 255, 257, 260
precaution   1
precise 180
precision   178
prefer 49, 87, 135, 144, 153, 173, 206, 273
preferably   175
preference   26, 173
preferred   215
premiums   261
prepare   11-12, 65, 83, 110, 133, 161, 215, 217, 226, 236,
244, 249-250, 257
prepared   12, 48, 52, 133, 141, 151
preparing   57, 63
presence   31, 148, 238
present   13, 68, 115, 119, 136, 149, 151, 159, 162, 171, 216-
217, 241, 248
president   19, 259, 264
pressure   65, 107, 117, 131, 143, 162, 182, 224, 228, 230,
238, 243, 278
pressured   29, 223, 280
pressures   79, 147
prevent   87
preventing   258
previous   12, 22, 48, 155, 172, 175, 200, 203, 211, 225, 242,
253, 259, 268
previously   44, 80, 149
primarily   207, 224
primary   114, 116
principles   68
priorities   3, 45, 68, 71, 79, 124, 163, 166, 208, 225, 227-228,
235, 241, 252, 266, 270, 273, 289, 292-293
prioritize   64, 137, 154, 230, 292
priority 9-10, 196
problem   2-3, 10, 13, 21, 34-35, 38, 40-42, 47, 50-51, 54, 67,
69, 73, 75, 84, 89-91, 93, 98, 105, 110, 117, 127, 136, 145, 176,
178, 180, 185, 194, 197-198, 208, 226-227, 231, 236, 242, 244, 255-
257, 259, 263, 267-268, 274, 292
problems   25, 39, 43-44, 51-52, 63, 68, 88, 98, 101, 130, 141,
149, 177-178, 186, 194, 197-198, 232-233, 235, 239, 245, 256, 260,
270, 277
procedure   8, 96, 180, 199, 229, 236, 258, 276
procedures   4, 34, 52, 55, 62-63, 100, 144, 237, 280, 287
proceed   42, 259

CPSIA information can be obtained
at www.ICGtesting.com
Printed in the USA
LVHW011834040822
725212LV00007B/91